STUDIES IN MODERN EUROPEAN LITERATURE
AND THOUGHT

General Editor:
E R I C H H E L L E R
Professor of German
in the University College of Swansea

M I S T R A L

MISTRAL

BY

ROB LYLE

NEW HAVEN
YALE UNIVERSITY PRESS
1953

Dedicated to

FÉLICIA LYLE

I

The traveller who crosses the English Channel, passes over the monotonous plain of Northern France, visits the airy mass of Chartres perhaps, or the luminous bubble of stone that is Vézelay, and journeys through the turretted hills of Burgundy will find, as at last he leaves Lyons behind him, that he has entered another world. He will have experienced a change more profound than any which preceded it. The air will have undergone a subtle transformation, will be sweeter and more radiant; the hills will present a clearer line, the buildings a sharper edge; the girls will be plumper, darker, more full of laughter; and visibly or invisibly he will be accompanied, henceforward, by the Rhône.

But his most striking illumination will come when he approaches the heart of this country of Provence which he has entered: and for this moment nature and man have combined to provide an appropriate setting. The Roman arch at Orange is the gateway to the 'sweet South', the gateway to both the southern clime and the blazing clarity of the Latin mind. For nowhere else is the Roman contribution to the splendour of our world made apparent with such a living and immediate physical impact.

This country is one of the anvils upon which Mediterranean civilization was hammered out. Inhabited originally by the Ligurians, it knew the Phoenician traders, and the Phoceans whose leader, Phocis, fell in love, according to the legend, with the beautiful daughter of a local chieftain, Gyptis. Their descendants, the Massaliots, summoned the aid of the Roman legions in their struggle with the Ligurians. The land became the *Provincia Romana* and saw Hannibal, and the barbarians; and legend tells how to its shores there sailed one day the Ship of the Saints, bearing from the Holy Land the Holy Marys, and Lazarus, and Sarah the black Saint of the Gypsies, bringing the light of the Cross to outshine the brilliance of Greece and Rome.

The Emperor Lothaire raised Provence to the status of a kingdom on the fall of the Hohenstaufens; in 1245, it was acquired by the family of Anjou, who retained it until 1487, when Charles VIII incorporated it into the kingdom of France. Its great city of Avignon had already housed the Popes, had witnessed the indomitable spirit of St Catherine of Siena, suffered the Black Death and the Inquisition, and was later to shelter the Stuarts; while close by, on the slopes of Mont Ventoux, Petrarch once meditated, rather priggishly, on the nature of life and love.

It is important to realise that this country has never been truly French: the change of atmosphere that our traveller experienced was not merely an effect of climate, still less of imagination. Even

Spain has left its mark here, for the Via Aurelia, which ran from Rome to Cadiz, passed through the city of Arles, itself an important post during the Saracenic invasion. At the same time, for historical and geographical reasons, Provence never attained to a truly individual existence. Now, we are apt to think of it as a land of romance, the home of the Troubadours and the Courts of Love, as indeed it was: and we are apt to forget that it was also a centre where the Mediterranean peoples intermingled, a place tempered by continual strife, and swept by historical winds as fierce as the mistral which whistles across its sparse plains and barren alps.

The results of this turbulent life can be seen and studied to-day in the features of the women of Provence, and more particularly in those of the women of Arles. I have before me an old photograph of one such miracle of nature, as I write. Her face has the soft but firm line of the Greek, and with the traditional Greek fairness of skin; a nobility of profile that was, and still is, Roman; a rich and smouldering fullness that is Spanish; a delicacy of feature and a refinement that is wholly French.

It is this very racial and temperamental mixture, thus expressed in the face of an *Arlésienne*, that makes of Provence a window through which one may observe the Latin mind. For the Mediterranean is prolific and diverse; the Italian and the Spaniard, the Berber and the Greek, differ profoundly. The essential quality which they have in common is obscured by existential differences. The forces which have produced and refined these distinct races, and caused these differences, have played less fiercely, or less effectively, on the people of Provence, with the result that we have something that is not 'Provençal', and yet belongs nowhere else; something, in short, that is truly 'Mediterranean' and 'Latin'.

At the same time this very quality hindered the country's adequate self-expression. Even the Troubadours, popularly the creators of a Provençal literature, wrote in a synthetic language. It was a literary language, a refinement or 'highest common factor' of the many variants of the Langue d'Oc spoken in the several districts of the Midi. This language came into being with Guillaume de Poictiers, in the eleventh century, and it died with the Middle Ages to which it belongs. Subsequent poets, writing in Langue d'Oc, wrote in whatever variant of that tongue happened to prevail in their own district; they certainly did not attempt to follow in the tradition of the Troubadours. The Langue d'Oc, one of the oldest of the Romance languages, had become a peasant *patois*. It was left to literary Romanticism—as always concerning itself with what is remote and 'unreal'—to reawaken interest in the neglected tongue: its protagonists turned nostalgically to the Middle Ages for inspiration, and unearthed the Troubadours; while their interest in folk-lore served to revive

6

their interest in the language in which it was expressed. From the beginning of the nineteenth century, Provençal writers are numerous, if not very memorable: the most notable among them being Diouloufet of Aix; the Marquis de la Fare-Alais; the baker's son from Marseilles, Victor Gelu; and the hairdresser from Ajen who possessed the poetic name of Jasmin.

These writers and poets, with others like them, were the pioneers in a revival that, if we except the harshly realistic Gelu, was essentially Romantic. The mixture of forces and elements already noted was the very factor which, while giving to Provence its unique character, prevented its individual expression. The coherent history and culture which produce a living national epic, such as in Spain is *El Cid*, in Lithuania *Pan Tadeusz*, or in Croatia *Judita*, was wanting to Provence; only a small minority possessed a national, historic consciousness, as opposed to a regional prejudice; and even now, when the revival has passed its climax and found its glorious fulfilment, its language still belongs to the few, a declining force even among the peasantry, and virtually ignored by the bourgeoisie.

If, however, such a national apotheosis were not to be expected, there was the promise, subsequently fulfilled, of an epic literature which would be truly Mediterranean just because it was truly Provençal: it was also natural that, when this came, it should have a nostalgic and valedictory quality. All epics tend to be heroic laments, summaries of, or funeral orations upon, the days that are no more, carrying with them the implication that such wonders and glories will never be again: but, in this case, the wonders and the glories, if they had not passed away, were visibly dying: Provence did not possess, and could not have produced, its Augustus or its Virgil.

It was to find a different kind of voice. On May 21st, 1854, an association of poet-patriots calling itself the Felibrige came into being. For its head and inspiration it had a great Provençal and a great European poet, who bore the name of the mighty wind that sweeps his country for half the year: Mistral.

II

The tree-lined road that can be seen stretching southwards, through the triumphal arch at Orange, leads to the shining city of Avignon. Avignon is shut off from Arles, to the south-west, by the rocky blue line of the Alpilles. Just to the north of this range is Maillane, and a little way to the south of this village lies the Mas du Juge, the farm-house where, on the feast of Our Lady's Nativity, 1830, Frédéric Mistral was born.

Frédéric was the autumnal fruit of his father's second marriage. In his book of memoirs, *Moun Espelido*, Mistral describes

7

how his father, François, met Delaïde, the young daughter of the mayor of Maillane, working in the fields at harvest: he likens the scene to that of the meeting of Ruth and Boaz. Six months after this meeting the couple were married.

François is a character of extraordinary grandeur, 'brought up and educated, like the Provençaux of old, in the Roman tradition': he was to leave an indelible impression on the mind of his son, and is immortalised in the patriarchs of Mistral's epics. This man, who would have been equally at home in Genesis, or Hesiod, or Homer, was the stern but just ruler of his rustic kingdom.

Frédéric's childhood was idyllic and his development was nurtured by a patriarchal tradition of immense antiquity whose ancient ways and wisdom the forces of progress threatened but had not then overthrown:

How gay it was, that world of rustic works! Each season renewed the cycle of labours. The ploughing, the sowing, the shearing, the mowing, the silkworms, the reaping, the threshing, the picking and gathering of the olives, spread out before my eyes the majestic motions of the agricultural life, always hard, but always calm and free.

A whole race of servants, of labourers hired by the month or the day, of weeders, and of haymakers, came and went on the farm, carrying on their shoulders goads or pitchforks or rakes, and worked always with noble gestures, as in the paintings of Léopold Robert.

When, for dinner or supper, one after another, they entered the farmhouse, and sat down, each according to his rank, round the great table, with my father at the head, he would gravely ask them questions and make his observations, on the flocks, the weather, and the work of the day, if things had been well, if the earth were hard or soft or in good order. Then, the meal over, the first carter closed the blade of his knife and all rose at once.

My father dominated all these country people by his stature, by his judgement, and by his nobility. He was a great and beautiful old man, dignified in his speech, kindly to the poor world, harsh only to himself.

Appropriately too, this patriarch was a man of profound faith. He had lived too near to life not to feel and reverence its majesty and wonder, and he who had read but three books, the Bible, the *Imitation of Christ*, and *Don Quixote*, was too wise and too perceptive not to feel humility. Mistral has described how each evening, winter and summer, he would kneel on a chair, head bare and hands crossed, and read the prayers to the assembled company: but it was at Christmas that the fervent glow of his

8

character was most fully felt. In reading Mistral one is constantly reminded of another great and reverent lover of life, Rubens; and the poet's description, in his memoirs, of a typical Christmas at his home has all the warmth and colour of a Rubens canvas.

On Christmas Day, the labourers would stop work early. Mistral's mother would give each one a girdle-cake, a round of nougat, a bunch of dried figs, a cheese, a celery salad, and a bottle of wine, before they returned to their own homes and families. Then the family and those who had no relatives would set out in search of the Yule-log which, traditionally, must come from a fruit-tree. In file, they would return with it to the farm, and circle the kitchen three times, after which François, pouring a glass of wine over the log, would recite a verse giving thanks to God. Then they would sit down to table. 'Oh! the sacred board, truly sacred, with, all around it, the whole family, happy and at peace . . .' There would follow the meal, with snails, fried cod and grey mullet with olives, artichokes, peppered celery, a plate of sweets—thick girdle-cakes in oil, dried raisins, almond nougat—and then, on top of all, the loaf which was never cut until a quarter had religiously been given to the first poor person who passed by. 'The evening, waiting for midnight mass, was long on that day; and round the fire there was lengthy talk of ancestors and much praise of their actions. But little by little, and willingly, my good father would return to Spain and to his memories of the siege of Figueras.'

Mistral's childhood was passed in an atmosphere of harmony and sanity which was later to bear fruit in his verse. The world, in its tragi-comic presumption, has been content to see this way of life succumb and wither, without protest. This life was perhaps stern, rigid, and unbending; it was rooted in tradition and hedged about with custom and ritual. Even the simplest meal was—as it should be—ritualistic. The law of man was subject to a higher law: the community was balanced and harmonious and therefore healthy. That this society was justified is proved by the people it produced—the lovely men and women—and the individuals of real grandeur of character, like Mistral's father; by the life which it enabled them to live; and, not least, by the production of a literature of which Mistral's work is the crowning glory.

It is idle to lament the passing of this life, for it is becoming an historical fact: much more vital is the fact that the values which it enshrined and preserved have been jettisoned or are in jeopardy. For this purpose, no substitute has been found; it is only now, on the edge of the abyss, beginning to be sought. This ritual, this orderliness and discipline, this devotion to custom, was not simply habit; it had a profound purpose, to enable men to live together in the fullest expression of their qualities and powers. It succeeded because, being fundamentally religious, it

9

could recognise that the individual person is sacred, while, at the same time, it was humble enough to realise that he is continually at the mercy of his own fallen nature. With much shouting and self-glorification, the prophets of progress, the pundits of infinite knowledge, the professional radicals, the merely greedy, announced the release of mankind from the chains of ignorance and superstition. They succumbed to the silliest superstition of all—that God is made in the image of man—and forged for themselves the terrible chains of that presumptuous licence which is the mockery of liberty.

That way of life cannot return as it was; but return it must, in a form appropriate to the time. Its structure and its fruits can, however, be studied; for, fortunately, its Latin harmony, the flower of Christian civilization, found immortal expression in the works of the poet whom it brought forth.

Frédéric Mistral's early schooling was in keeping with this background. At the age of eight he was sent to St Michel-de-Frigolet, an establishment run by a certain M. Donat who, very sensibly, was more interested in play and happiness than in work. Unfortunately, this gay institution went the way of all flesh, and, at the age of thirteen, Mistral was sent to the Collége Royal d'Avignon. Here he was subjected to two decisive influences. First, he found himself among people who spoke French, and despised him for his regional accent (at home he spoke the dialect) and for his country ways; and here, also, he met the college usher, Roumanille.

The first experience touched his pride and, because his upbringing had been of that traditional kind which forms character, its effect was to stimulate his innate independence and his interest in the speech and customs of his people which were to lead both to his writings and to his public life as a regionalist.

The meeting with Roumanille belongs to a different order of experience: it represents that moment in the creative life when all which before was confused aspiration becomes inspired purpose. There is a break in the clouds, and the stars without which one can voyage no further can clearly be seen. Joseph Roumanille was twelve years older than Mistral; 'a young professor with a fine black beard', and a gifted lyric poet of delicacy and pastoral simplicity. One day he found Mistral translating the penitential psalms into Provençal and thereupon recited a group of his own lyrics: 'a true blossoming of April flowers', writes Mistral, 'of wild flowers, flowers prophetic of the felibrean spring which ravished me until I exclaimed to myself: Here is the dawn for which my soul was waiting so that it might open to the light!'

Roumanille initiated Mistral into the mysteries of his own poetic art, and recited to him the work of Jasmin, the Marquis de la Fare-Alais, and Gelu: for him, poetry and morality and religion must go hand in hand: the purest vision will come of the purest Faith. The climax of his teaching was: 'Always be a good christian, my boy, the rest will come for certain. And never forget that the best day of your life is that of your first communion!' Profoundly religious, Roumanille had at this time less faith in the future of Provence and its language. A few years afterwards, he would have this too, and it would be implanted in him by his pupil.

Three years later Mistral went to the University of Aix, to study law. He graduated in 1851. In the meantime he had been writing verse, including a long poem in four cantos, *Li Meissoun*, a kind of *Georgics*, but written in the manner of the *Chanson de Roland*, and showing a first-hand knowledge of the countryside. Some of the shorter poems of this period were published in 1852, in an anthology, *Li Prouvençalo;* but Mistral's poetic and public life really began after he had left the University.

III

In 1851, Mistral started to write *Mirèio*. This poem was not completed until 1858, when he gave the first reading of it to a group of friends, including the poet Aubanel who, as a critic has said, is to Mistral what Catullus was to Virgil. It is the first, and perhaps the finest flower of that civilization into which he was born and in which he grew up.

Mirèio is an epic, the poem of a country and a people, but it is a rustic epic: its Achilles is a poor and humble young man, the son of a wandering basket-maker, and its Helen a simple country girl, the daughter of a farmer. It is written in twelve books, and composed in an original seven-line stanza, in the first of which the poet is at pains to explain that he is attempting to do for Provence what Homer did for Greece, and at the same time to make clear that he is to do this, not through some exalted character, 'with golden diadem and damask mantle', but, as befits one who 'sings only for you, shepherds and people of the farms', through the person of a typical maiden of his beloved countryside, in whom it is not difficult to see a recollection of that young girl whom his father wooed, the mayor's daughter, standing alone amid the alien corn:

A maiden of Provence I sing.
In the love of her youth's spring,
A simple, country girl whom now,
Though to the outside world unknown,
By Homer's great example borne
I wish to trace, amid the corn,
Towards the sea, across the Crau.[1]

1 For the original Provençal of this and the following translations (which are all by Rob Lyle), see Appendix, page 58.

This introduction is followed by an invocation to Christ, 'born among shepherds', from whom is all inspiration, and to whom the poet's prayer rises, that, like the birds, on the wings 'of our Provençal tongue', he may attain to that branch whose fruits lie beyond the reach of the pickers. Then the tale begins.

Mèste Ambròsi, the basket-maker, and his son, Vincèn, ask hospitality at the *Mas di Falabrego*, the Farm of the Mulberries, where Mirèio, daughter of Mèste Ramoun, makes them welcome. Mèste Ambròsi is prevailed upon by the farm-labourers to sing an old ballad, and Vincèn, questioned by Mirèio, tells of youthful sports and contests. As a result, love opens in her heart, as sweetly and naturally as a flower in spring.

Between our world and Mirèio's, Freud has let fall the cold fog of his puritanical analysis, and has reduced to the dead level of sexual appetite the sharp peaks of youthful passion, with their snow-caps of sunlit joys and their *alpenrot* of transitory despairs. For, in Mirèio's world, though they be touched with the shadow of Original Sin, its characters are not yet warped by the revolt of a much greater presumption; theirs is a world wherein it is permitted to children to be young, and to old men to be wise. And what delightful children they are; this Mirèio:

> Fifteen summers had Mirèio—
> And the blue coast of Font-Vieio,
> You hills of Baux, you plains of Crau,
> You've never seen such loveliness!
> The sun had granted it such grace,
> And, fresh and innocent, her face
> With dimpled cheeks like flowers did blow.
>
> Her look was dew upon the leaf
> That dissipates all sign of grief—
> Starlight is less sweet and pure:
> It shone in those black locks whose flow
> Fashioned its ringlets on her brow
> And her rounded breast was now
> A double peach, still immature.

and this Vincèn:

> Vincèn was not as yet sixteen
> But in his form and face was seen
> Fine youth, and promise in his glance—
> Burned brown, it's true . . . but the black earth
> To the best vintage will give birth
> And from the raisin dark as dearth
> There comes the wine to make you dance.

These children are real beings: persons. We have met them, however briefly, in the surroundings of Mistral's own upbringing. They are not the ideals of a romantic imagination, or the compensating symbols of a 'reactionary' dreamer. When, in the second canto, Mirèio and Vincèn declare their love for each other, in one of the most delicately sweet love-scenes in all literature, they do so with all the reverent eagerness of people imbued with the idea that one's neighbour is uniquely and irreplaceably valuable; they do so with a kind of awe at this perennial but ever fresh exposure of divinity—the eternal love and grace—somehow manifesting itself under the symbols of dark eyes, and red lips, and the inexplicable tenderness of line which defines the onset of human passion, that sweet cry in the ominous hush of our existence whose echoes sound through the eternal silences, for ever and ever.

This scene, of pure enchantment, is introduced, and interrupted, by a refrain which delicately paints in the background to the human drama; for it is the time of the mulberry-picking:

> Sing, *magnanarello*, sing!
> For to harvest is to sing!
> The silkworm its third crop secretes;
> The mulberry trees are full of girls,
> Round whom the sunny weather swirls—
> A flight of golden bees that whirls
> To rob the rosemary of its sweets!

Mistral is particularly happy in his landscapes and scene-painting, and he is sensitive to every mood and variation of nature, but, unlike many northern poets, he does not exalt nature at the expense of man; for him the human being is the centre of creation, and his nature-poetry nearly always exists only to enhance a human situation, or provide a setting appropriate to some play of character which occupies the foreground.

In the next canto, devoted to the talk of the women, the background is the gathering of the cocoons which the silk-worms have spun. The range of reference is wide, and touches many aspects of Provençal history and geography: it ends with the singing of the ballad of *Magali*, which has all the quality of an original folk-song.

In the third canto, the time was spring: in the fourth it is summer, and, as if with the growing heat, the drama intensifies. Three suitors appear, to beg Mirèio's hand; and the first is a shepherd, Alàri.

Mistral exploits the introduction of Alàri to describe him, as he leads his huge herd of sheep up to the hill-pastures, crook in hand and with his white sheep-dogs, a dignified figure from the pastoral age, biblical and timeless, in one of those superb pictures which remind one of Rubens.

13

The second suitor is Véran, the *gardian*, or herdsman, of the Camargue, and through him we are given a vision of the wild horses of the plain, which roam there to this day, watched over by the cowboys with their tridents, or triple-pronged lances.

Finally, there comes the *toucadou*, Ourrias, the breeder of fighting bulls. In stanzas of great vigour, Mistral describes the rounding up of the herd for branding; the epic contest between Ourrias and one of the bulls, which he eventually overturns by the horns; and his final goring, by another bull, which leaves him with a long and sinister scar.

While each suitor has been used to elaborate on an aspect of Provençal life, the story has been suspended: but each suitor is rejected, and with the refusal of Ourrias, it begins to move forward quickly again. For, unlike the others, Ourrias cannot reconcile himself to the blow.

Angry and sullen, he turns homeward over the desolate Crau. There he meets Vincèn, coming towards him: Ourrias insults him, and they fight. Ourrias is beaten, but when Vincèn spares him Ourrias treacherously strikes him with his trident and leaves him for dead. He hurries on his way which leads him to the banks of the Rhône. Crossing in the ferry, he sees, upon the further bank, the St Medard's night procession, composed of the souls of those who have been drowned in the river: and he too must drown, for it is a phantom boat in which he is crossing and it slowly sinks beneath him.

The fight between Vincèn and Ourrias is characteristic of Mistral's reading of life. His hero must be a man and prove worthy of his beloved; for, in that world, lovely girls desire marriage, and a large family, and fine sons. The epic hero is usually, of necessity, almost super-human, a man of destiny, for he must be a symbol as well as a leader of men. In *Mirèio*, Mistral combines, in Vincèn, the qualities required of an epic hero with those common to any spirited young man of his country. In that vision of the world which the Mediterranean seems to impose on its sons, the keynote is clarity. Line and colour combine to limit, to order, to define. The individual takes on a special significance, and his functions are more precisely ordered than elsewhere. It is the same with the person's relations with his neighbour: these too must be clarified; each must have his place and his function, for the ultimate aim is harmony, between men and men, between men and women, between man and nature, between man and God. Hence Vincèn, who defeats evil in the form of Ourrias, is not acting in an exceptional way, for the sake of a literary tradition: he is reflecting, idealistically if you will, a code of action, a code of honour, characteristic of his race and of the Catholic culture of which he is the product. Mistral on to the old epic tradition of the Aegean has grafted the shoot of a living religious ethos, filling out the form of the classical hero with the richer

14

content of the Christian interpretation of man; with the Roman reading of life.

In the same way, he follows the usual device of introducing the supernatural into his narrative, but, in place of the ancient Gods—to which even as late as Camoëns the epic poet had recourse—he introduces Christian mysticism, in this episode of the crossing of the Rhône, combined with a local religious tradition, so that, while attaching himself to an ancient literary precedent, he contrives to give it a Christian form, at the same time localising it by reference to a folk-belief characteristic of his own country.

Vincèn is found by swineherds and carried back to the farm. The sixth canto tells how he is restored to health by the witch, Taven, who lives in a cave in the Alpilles. It is a characteristic record of local legend and folk-lore, which, however, somewhat holds up the action.

This is resumed in the next canto, wherein Vincèn prevails upon his father to visit Mèste Ramoun and ask, on his son's behalf, for Mirèio's hand. He arrives at the farm with a group of harvesters, and all are royally entertained by the master. When these two old men, so like each other in many ways, and both of them made in the image of the poet's remarkable father, François,[1] are finally alone, Ambròsi has his say; the suit is rejected.

This set-back, so necessary to the whole story, is the one romantic element in the poem, and is reminiscent of that Troubadour tradition which insisted that the highest love is unsatisfied and frustrated by circumstance, if not by the will of its protagonists, as is the case in the legend of Tristram and Iseult.

Ambròsi departs: night falls: and the canto closes with another scene worthy of Rubens. It is Midsummer night, the night of St John, patron of harvest; and round the blazing log fire the harvesters dance the farandole in honour of their patron saint:

> With proud heads high and free of care,
> Tumbling in the vibrant air,
> As one, they jumped and struck the ground
> As into the farandole they sped.
> The great flame crackled and was spread
> To strike reflections from each head
> By the great wind that whirled around.
>
> A swirl of sparks soars furiously
> Like unleashed stars, into the sky,

---

[1] 'I have portrayed him in my poem under two different forms, *Mèste Ambròsi et Mèste Ramoun*. I have not put into these two characters of old men, I have not attributed to them a single word that I had not seen in my old father, or heard from his mouth.' (from a letter to Adolphe Dumas.)

As in the flame the fire-wood tumbles,
  While mingling with the tumult goes
  The gay and playful flute that blows
  Like a tree-sparrow in the boughs—
St John, for you the pregnant country trembles!

  The furnace sparked and danced with joy,
  The tambourine monotonously
Droned, buzzed and muttered like the sea
  When in the deep with peaceful beat
  It murmurs round earth's rocky feet,
  While the burned dancers, dark with heat,
Brandished their shining blades on high.

  Then, with enormous jumps, three times
  They fire off muskets through the flames
And over the red blaze they gyre,
  While from one tress of corn they glean the
  Husks into the dying ember
  Clasping St John's Wort and verbena,
Blessed in the purifying fire:

  'St John! St John! St John!' they cried.
  And then it seemed the hills had died
And stars through all the shades were pouring,
  The while a wilful gust had brought
  Air from the hills with incense fraught
  Which, with the glow the fire had wrought,
Through the blue dusk towards the Saint went soaring.

These descriptive frescos are common in Mistral, especially
in his early work. The poet has constructive power of an unusual
order for, while he builds up his scenes with many realistic details, these are successfully subordinated to the whole, which, at
the end, emerges vivid and complete, standing out in the mind's
eye like a piece of sculpture. Mistral has applied the plastic
genius of the south, its visual sense and its sense of form, which
is almost tactile, to poetry, the art of time, with marvellous results. Only Dante, among poets, excels him in this quality; but
Dante's method, and his purpose, are quite different.

Meanwhile, Mirèio remembers Vincèn's advice, to call on the
aid of *Li Santo*, the Holy Marys, if ever she be in trouble. She
decides to set out, and leaves the house secretly. The eighth
canto describes the first part of her journey across the barren
Crau, a place of pitiless heat and waterless wastes. Eventually
she comes across some Rhône fishermen who shelter her for the
night.

Back at the farm, Mèsté Ramoun has discovered her absence.

He organises a search, sending a runner to ask news of all the labourers. By this perfectly logical device, we are given a picture of the whole farm and all who work on it, for the runner passes from the mowers to the ploughmen, from the ploughmen to the harvesters, and ends up, on the boundaries of the farm, with the solitary shepherds, keeping watch over their flocks. One old shepherd saw Mirèio pass by before dawn, and heard the name of *Li Santo* on her lips. Her parents, hearing this, set off in pursuit.

This ninth canto is a marvel of observation, organisation, and description, a feast of colour and energy. At the same time it is formally perfect: nothing is introduced which is not appropriate to the theme and to the development of the central drama. Each scene, each episode, is even linked, as in a piece of music, by the recurring refrain of the runner's anxious question.

But Mirèio has crossed the Rhône, to continue her terrible journey. She sets out again in the early morning, sped on her way by the fisherman, and surrounded by the sweetness of the dawn upon the great river, which forms a poetic, and pitiless, contrast to the horror of heat which is to follow:

> As he was speaking, on the Rhône,
> Resplendent with the rosy tone
> Shed by the morning light; the barges
> Sailed slowly up, and from the sea
> The wind with their white sails grew free
> And pressed them on, as easily
> As shepherdess her snowy charges.

She passes on into the flat waste, among the tamarisks, and the cruel mirage. She has sunstroke, but fortified by the sight of the distant sea, at last she reaches the church, Les Saintes Maries de la Mer, and flinging herself down and summoning her last reserves of strength, calls upon the Saints:

> O Holy Marys dear,
> Who can change the tear
> Into the flower,
> Hear my prayer
> In this dark hour!
>
> Alas! when you will see
> My great agony
> And all my care,
> You will comfort me
> With piteous air.
>
> I am a young girl
> Who loves a boy,

17

Vincèn the beautiful!
Dear Saints I love him, he
Is all my joy.

I love him! I love him
Even as the rill
Delights to run,
Or the strong bird will
Soar in the sun.

They would that I extinguish.
This fire so strong and free
That does not wish to perish!
They would I should not cherish
The flowering almond-tree!

O Holy Marys dear,
Who can change the tear
Into the flower,
Hear my prayer
In this dark hour!

I have come from far
To find peace here.
Crau nor heath could bar
My steps, nor mother's care
Could hold me there!

And the sun so fierce is,
I feel his rays like rain
Of nails and a great pain,
As though with thorns he pierces
My burning brain.

But, have faith in what I say!
Give me my Vincèn;
When, full of joy and gay
We will both come back then,
To see you once again.

O the throbbing in my brain
Will no longer burn;
The tears that tumble down like rain
And my looks with sorrow stain
To shining joy will turn.

This joy that joins us two
My father won't behold:

To touch him where he's cold
Isn't much to ask of you,
Lovely Saints of gold!

For though the olive on the hill
May grow up hard and bent
And seem immutable—
The wind that blows at Advent
Matures it when it will.

The medlar and the rowan,
So bitter when one starts
To cut, need but be shaken,
A little grass be taken
To soften their hard hearts!

O Holy Marys dear,
Who can change the tear
Into the flower,
Hear my prayer
In this dark hour!

Mirèio's prayer is answered by the appearance of the Marys
who come to bring her comfort and strength and, to this end,
tell her, in the eleventh canto, the story of their own troubles,
of their persecution in the Holy Land, their long journey to
Provence, and their conversion of her country.

Once again, Mistral is able to use the passionate and un-
complicated faith of his countrymen and women to raise his
narrative to another level of experience, illuminating the old
and worn-out mechanism of epic powers with a delicate Christian
mysticism.

Meanwhile, Mirèio's parents have arrived and found her in
a state of collapse. She is carried up to the roof, where are the
relics of the Saints. At last Vincèn too arrives from over the
Crau. Torn with grief he kneels at her side and she welcomes
him, trying, because she is herself consoled by her vision, to
comfort him. The chant of the attendants rises, and Mirèio has
her last vision: the Marys appear, borne over the blue waves of
the Mediterranean in their boat that carries no sail, to fetch her
away to eternal blessedness and the joyous contemplation of the
beatific vision. 'What is this death that daunts you, but a mist
that dissolves?'

She leaves a scene of weeping and lamentation which is finally
overwhelmed by the rising chant from the church below: 'If it
be peace that they need, the poor sinners who lament at your
door, O white flowers of our salted plains, give them peace in
abundance!'

From its first appearance this poem had an astonishing success; for it made no concessions to the spirit of the times. Its triumph in Provence was to be expected, but in Paris it was acclaimed by Adolphe Dumas, who likened its author to Virgil, and by Lamartine, who compared him with Homer. Its beauty and freshness have never faded: on the contrary, its popularity has constantly grown. Since its first triumph it has been translated into more than a dozen languages. And Mirèio herself has become a part of our civilized consciousness; another Antigone, another Beatrice, another Juliet; only 'un chato de Prouvenço', but a country maiden, for all that, of an unsurpassed purity, beauty, and heroism, who is, and must forever be, the shining symbol of the country in which she was conceived. The desert Crau had miraculously flowered again, and with the fairest flower of all.

IV

Mistral's first epic was published at Avignon in 1859; but he had been active in other ways during the period of its composition.

In 1852, a group of Provençal poets had met together at Arles, at the instigation of Mistral, Roumanille and Gaut. A similar meeting took place at Aix in the following year, and in 1854, at Font-ségugne, this association of poet-patriots was officially born, and baptised the Felibrige.

The foundation of the Felibrige marks the beginning of Mistral's political life, for this association carried with it patriotic as well as poetic implications. These were to emerge more clearly after the success of *Mirèio*, which conferred a sudden lustre and authority upon the group.

It was certainly required, for, with minor exceptions, the Provençal poets of the time were undistinguished: they needed, above all things, the leadership and example of genius. There was, too, some confusion in the growth of the movement. The great Romantics embraced the cause of regionalism principally for political reasons—the tendency dates from 1848—and, with characteristic inconsistency, sentimentalised over 'worker-poets'; although their leader, Reboul, while not much of a poet, was a passionate adherent of the cause of Henri V.

Mistral's attitude, by contrast, is from the start entirely consistent, and he moves step by step in the formulation of his *politik*. From the beginning he is, then, a regionalist, desiring to see put into effect that degree of decentralization which will preserve local language, custom, and tradition. He is therefore in opposition to the Empire. At the same time he has vision: he is not a separatist. He understands very well that a chain is as strong as its weakest link; that the distinct provinces of a great country will be all the stronger, and more loyal, by virtue of their independence. The wise ruler, sure of his authority and position, can afford to allow his subjects a large measure of freedom, his peoples a large measure of autonomy; they will be all the healthier, all the more united, for these concessions. But the weak ruler, or the tyrant, must draw the reins of government (and he must work through a centralised bureaucracy) ever more tightly into his hands. Mistral, always balanced, clear, and serene, desired above all harmony, the equilibrium of conflicting forces for their individual and mutual benefit. Thus he was, to all intents and purposes, a federalist.

The liberal opposition, to which Mistral was at that time attached, was overwhelmed in 1851, and only gradually recovered its force during the next fifteen years. In the meantime, he had written his second epic, *Calendau*, which was completed in 1866.

This poem is very different from *Mirèio*, and reflects Mistral's current preoccupation with political problems. It is much more a regional, even a nationalist, poem than *Mirèio*, and for that reason alone has never enjoyed the success of its predecessor: the action is continually suspended by historical and topographical digressions, delightful in themselves but injurious to the shape of the whole: no character with the actuality of Mirèio emerges, the persons are symbols rather than portraits, mouthpieces for a dissertation on the wines of the country, or the fish which can be caught round its coasts. At the same time it contains passages of superb poetry; stanzas of a fervour and sublimity unsurpassed in all the poet's work. We are plunged into one as we begin to read.

This time, it is a simple fisherman to whom we are introduced in the first stanza. The scene has moved from the farms and the pastures to the coast. Then, without pause, follows the great invocation to the soul of Provence:

> . . . *soul of my native land*

> You that flamed forth and came to be
> Both in her speech and history
> When German, Picard and Burgundian,
> Besieged Toulouse, and then Beaucaire,
> You who did kindle everywhere
> Against the dark invaders there
> Men of Marseilles and Avignon;

> You who by force of memory
> Preserved our hope in days to be,
> You who, despite the grave and death,
> Fairer, more fruitful, more on fire,
> Did still the Troubadours inspire,
> Rejuvenating sage and sire
> Till Mirabeau spoke with the mistral's breath;

... The inundations of the years
And all their tempests and their fears
In vain mix race and boundary;
For nature and the earth, our mother,
Will feed us, sister, son and brother,
With the same milk; their breasts discover
The good oil to the olive tree.

Soul eternally reborn,
Noble, joyful, full of scorn,
That in the Rhône and Rhône-wind neighs!
Great soul of the harmonious wood,
Of inlets where the sun's rays brood,
Dear soul of our Provençal blood,
I call thee! Live within my lays!

This passage is accompanied by a long and important note, which throws much light on the poet's outlook at the time, and reveals an interesting historical preoccupation which in all probability Mistral never abandoned, but which in any case is especially relevant to the composition of *Calendau*.

The line 'Quand li baroun picard, aleman, bourguignoun' is, as the note explains, a reference to the Albigensian crusade, which Mistral saw as an aggressive movement spurred on by racial rather than by religious feeling. He refers to the Crusaders as 'the invaders from the north'. The peoples of Languedoc, from the Alps to the Gulf of Gascony, from the Loire to the Ebro, have always been, the poet asserts, drawn together by a similarity of climate, instincts, customs, beliefs, law and language, with their nationality revealed and propagated by the Troubadours. One thing only was needed to effect a unity: a common enemy; but when, in crusader's dress, he appeared, he did so armed by the Church and in overwhelming force. The defeat of the peoples of Languedoc, as Mistral rightly notes, marked the beginning of the development of modern France; but he is insistent that these peoples desired rather a 'federal state', which is, to put it mildly, doubtful. Mistral is attributing to his ancestors national sentiments which were only born into consciousness in his own epoch. It is certain, however, that these peoples had a distinct existence, and, once this is granted, it is difficult not to agree with the poet's solution: but the federal idea, for which Mistral doubtless drew sustenance from the example of Alexander Hamilton, in America, and from the Swiss Republic, is a comparatively modern one, even today by no means accepted.

While, therefore, we may take exception to aspects of Mistral's historical interpretation, the principle upon which he has seized, and to which he adheres, is one which reveals him a practical visionary, and places him, politically, well in advance of his time. In the light of which, and before following him further along this road, we may return to the consideration of *Calendau*.

Calendau, the fisherman of Cassis, a little fishing-village near Toulon, loves Esterello, a girl of noble blood, a descendant of that race of eagles, *Les Baux*, who once lived in the eyrie of that name, now ruined, and, swooping from time to time from their heights like birds of prey, terrorised the surrounding countryside. A proud and daring race, not unlike a typical family of the Italian Renaissance—Gonzaga, or Este—they are described by Esterello in the first canto of the poem, together with other aspects of her history which, overflowing into the next canto, include her meeting and marriage with Lou Comte Severan, who turns out to be a bandit and a monster. From him, in horror, Esterello flees, by night, to take refuge in a cave in the mountains, and to be identified by local superstition with the fairy 'Esterello' (we are never told her real name) and, subsequently, to meet with Calendau, who, having heard all, sets out in search of the Count.

He crosses Provence, and his journey is used as a pretext to enlarge on the beauties of the country; its vistas; its hills, valleys and rivers; its trees and fruits. At last he meets with Severan, to whom he recounts the story of his life and exploits, with the object of provoking him.

'I am from Cassis, by the sea', he begins, and proceeds to describe it, not forgetting to mention its wine:

> Oh! could you taste it, you would see
> It's sweeter than the honey-bee,
> Scented with rosemary, diamond clear,
> The heather and myrtle that do grow
> Over our hills, enrich it so,
> It dances in the glass—I know
> I'd drain a flagon, were one here.

and to enumerate the fish which may be caught in its waters and the nets which are used to catch them. Every detail of the fishing is described, against the perfect backcloth of a summer night:

> It is a clear, a summer night:
> A whirl of stars falls from the height
> Into the deep; a lovelier arises.
> Soft to the oar the ocean grows
> And shimmering and sprawling flows
> And to the far horizon glows . . .
> It is a magic scene, that e'er surprises.

Calendau then speaks, in the fourth canto, of his father, and of Provence, home of his Ligurian ancestors: he tells of the Phoceans who brought to Provence the arts of civilization; of the Roman colonies at Agatha (Agde), Antipolis (Antibes), and Nicoa (Nice), and of Marseilles, whose inhabitants embraced the cause of Pompey against Caesar; of the coming of Christianity; of his country's independence and *effloraison* under the rival dynasties of the Raimonds de Toulouse and the Raimonds-Bérengers, when Provence, as Mistral tells us in a note, from the Midi to Catalonia, 'attained a degree of political independence, of literary culture, of religious tolerance, of elegant custom and of material prosperity, superior to the general condition of the rest of Europe'. This is Provence's Medicean or Periclean age. Then comes the Albigensian crusade, the invasion from the north, and the Inquisition. Provence—and the Provençal tongue—sustain a mortal blow.

Calendau then tells of his meeting with Esterello, of his declaration, and its rejection, and of his departure, determined to perform such deeds as will conquer this disdain.

His first labour (Calendau is the Hercules of Provence) is the acquisition of riches, by means of a fabulous fishing expedition, a descriptive opportunity which the poet exploits to the full. But Esterello is not satisfied: her suitor must learn the vanity of mere gold, and she draws his attention to the example of the Troubadours, of Rudel, Foulquet, Vidal, Guillaume de la Tour, whose prowess was of a purer and altogether more exalted nature.

The sixth canto, something of an intermezzo, shows us Cassis *en fête*. There follows a description of certain Provençal dances, *Li Courdello, Li Pastourello, Li Mouresco, Li Triho, Lis Ouliveto*, and, of course, *La Farandoulo*. In a note on these dances and their like, Mistral has this to say: '. . . our fathers excelled in clothing life with poetry. This idealisation of daily labour . . . contributed not a little to making each one love the condition and the country into which God had caused him to be born.'

This is a concrete and obvious example of an attitude to life typical of Mistral, which continually bears poetic fruit in the harmony and universality of so many of the episodes, descriptions and scenes in his epics. He is giving stylised expression to a world of experience, of thought, and of imagination, which itself is composed of countless stylised gestures. The poet himself, as we have seen, grew up against a background of such almost ritualistic gestures, of unconscious expressions of love, reverence, comradeship, compassion, interdependence, and hospitality, refined and hallowed by custom; no mere empty forms, but living conventions because illuminated by mutual trust and understanding, and by a common faith.

Nothing happens in isolation. The disintegration of the atom is paralleled by the disintegration of society and even of the human personality itself. Our society is collapsing for want of a common purpose and a common belief. Men can no longer speak

24

to each other, for want of common premises. They talk different languages and inhabit a Babel of the spirit; while our men of genius no longer speak for, or to, the people. Our society has become inarticulate because it has ceased to be a community.

A healthy communal life expresses itself, externalises its beliefs, feelings, hopes, fears, ambitions and sorrows, through the mediums of folk-song and folk-lore; communal dances; customs, especially those surrounding the great events of childbirth, marriage and death; the shared ritual of religion; and the folk-arts, such as embroidery, which may, as in the Balkans, express the whole soul of a people in terms of highly abstract and elaborate design.

But a community which presumes to abandon its beliefs, and, in defiance of religious restraint, sets no bounds to the acquisition of material prosperity, substituting a gullible and superstitious reverence for science for the belief of an immortal soul in a personal God, destroys itself. Our mechanical society, having thus made a God of Humanity, has forgotten how to sing, to dance, to worship, to love, to tell stories, to think—in short, to live—and, for self-expression, is reduced to the bald raising of a clenched fist, and the raucous reiteration of stereotyped slogans. Even at its most intelligent, it can only express itself, and then esoterically, in terms of a *Waste Land* or—climax of inverted buffoonery—a *Ulysses*.

Mistral, by contrast, has something different to offer: the sublimation, in terms of great and idealistic art, of a community as it should be, whole, healthy, and harmonious; giving permanent shape to its lineaments, concrete form to its ideals, and ardent expression to its latent aspirations. He was, of course, fortunate in his material; it lay ready to his hand; but the transmutation of base, if fine, metal into gold was his achievement; and when he spoke, he spoke for a people, a race, a way of life, and, ultimately, for Western civilization—born, like himself, of the Mediterranean—with as natural an expression as the dances which he describes through the mouth of his national hero Calendau.

Calendau, meanwhile, has gone on to describe the joust without which no such fête would be complete. This exciting sport, the descendant of the old Roman water-games, the *Naumachia*, is practised enthusiastically to this day. The protagonists face each other on floating platforms, raised high over the water and drawn by multi-oared barges: they are armed with long lances and, as they collide, attempt to 'unseat' each other. Team competes against team, each drawn from a port or fishing village.

Calendau emerges victorious and relates the story of his exploit to Esterello who, though this time visibly moved, exhorts him with a greater example—*Lis Aliscamp*, the battle fought by Guillaume au Court Nez against the Saracens, and named after the famous cemetery at Arles, said (probably by *un vrai Marseillais*) to have been blessed by Christ himself; it was celebrated in a thirteenth century French poem.

In the seventh canto, the hero sets out once more, this time to cut down the larches on Mont Ventoux, and, not content with that, to travel on to the Nesque valley, rob the hives of the Rocher du Cire of their honey and return with a portion of it to Esterello. She is not impressed and, quite rightly, rates him for undertaking tasks so destructive, even in the pursuit of glory.

Repentant, Calendau goes on a pilgrimage to the Sainte-Baume where he meets with two parties of the Compagnons du Tour de France, about to engage in a fight. He reconciles these representatives of ancient trades and at last succeeds in pleasing Esterello, who declares her love for him but, fearing that his may decline from a surfeit of happiness, sets before his eyes a still higher ideal: to rid the country of a monstrous bandit, Marco-mau, which exploit occupies the ninth canto.

He leads Marco-mau to Aix, in chains, and is received *coume un prince*, and fêted by the whole city, whose characteristically elaborate and symbolic pageant is minutely described. He ends his recitation with a peroration on pure love which enrages Severan, who takes him to his castle, the *Castelet d'Eiglun;* and, in the eleventh canto, called *The Orgy*, entices him with *un festin sardanapalen*. At last, outraged, Calendau overturns the table and challenges Severan to mortal combat, but one of the bandits fells him with a blow on the head and he is flung into a dungeon. He is helped to escape by a woman from Severan's band, and as the twelfth and last canto opens, hastens back to Esterello to defend her against Severan who has in the meantime set out to capture her. He returns by sea and passes by the islands of the coast, Les Iles de Lerius, and Les Iles d'Or, near Hyères with its oranges and pomegranates, *Coume un Jardin dis Esperido;* isles as remotely beautiful as a scene from Homer, heavy with legend, lying in the brilliant blue sea, hazy and nostalgic, with the pines leaning down over the waters of their gentle bays; isles heady with the scent of herbs, and loud with the sawing of the cicadas. Passing Toulon, he at last sights Lou Gibau and that coast of olives and oaks and terebinths 'where the wave fringes the golden beach with silver', the site of the parent town of Marseilles, the Greek city of Taurentum. He reaches Esterello, and, uttering a superb invocation, which begins:

> Trees of Mount Gibau! Pines, and you
> Myrtle-woods, juniper, and yew!
> And you, O sunset! you, O heath so calm!
> Great ocean! In my agony
> I take you, now, as testimony—
> Witness my love's eternity! . . .
> Birds of the forest, sing my wedding psalm!

he prepares to meet Severan's assault, hurling rocks down the mountainside until the bandit is at last consumed in the flames of the burning pine forests to which he himself has set fire.

V

Such a bare description of the action is sufficient to show the elaboration of incidental detail in this poem, and to point the difference from Mistral's earlier epic. This attention to description not essential to the action in fact violates one of the first principles of the epic form, which asserts that everything must be subordinated to the narrative. We miss here the harmonious perfection of *Mirèio*, its symmetry and frieze-like shape, so vital and plastic that it seems almost tangible. We miss too those great carved tableaux, in which time seems to stand still and a multitude of actions appear almost simultaneously before our eyes, so perfectly organised is the material. Not least, we miss the revelation of human character. The leading figures in *Calendau* are little more than ciphers, mouthpieces for passionate meditations on every aspect of the poet's beloved country. For these reasons it can perhaps never have the universal appeal—as it has certainly never had the success—of its predecessor. When that is said, however, it remains a tremendous achievement, a national hymn of great power, with passages of unsurpassed poetry, and with informative descriptions of scenes and customs of a luminous precision.

To read and understand *Calendau* adequately one must have a knowledge of its background, of the development of Mistral's mind at the time: and the political aspirations which went to its making were to find clarification in action soon after its publication.

The liberal opposition had by now recovered its strength, and in January, 1867, Mistral left Avignon for Paris with Victor Balaguer, the Catalan poet, who was going to join the Spanish liberals. Mistral, for his part, went to join the republican opposition, desiring to see the fall of Napoleon III and to work for the establishment of a federal France, under a republic, which he believed would ensure to his own people the rights which they sought.

Mistral had for long been sympathetic towards the aspirations of the Catalonians, and in his correspondence is at pains to draw parallels between the development of the two countries. There was a distinct similarity between the French and Spanish Republicans; between Spanish provincial separatism and the Commune; and between the Carlist cause and that associated with the Comte de Chambord. Mistral, however, as Marius André notes, reached a different conclusion from Balaguer and Quintana.

27

They were die-hard liberals, but Mistral, better able to learn from events, turned gradually towards those ideas of order and authority, traditionally Mediterranean, and associated with the causes of Legitimacy and of Catholicism.

But this was to come later. On this first trip to Paris, with Balaguer, he had little if any faith in a restoration of the legitimate monarchy. He departed with the hopes and exhortations of his revolutionary allies ringing in his ears. Soon after, he returned to Maillane, not in triumph, or to engage in renewed party politics, but quietly, and to undertake a very different task: the compilation of a dictionary of all the dialects of the Midi.

The explanation of his obvious disillusionment is to be found partly in the poet's inexperience, and partly in the meaning which we give to the word 'revolution'. The politicians, the heirs of 1792, may have welcomed the disruptive assistance of a regionalist so long as they remained in opposition but, the Republic once proclaimed, with all its bureaucratic and centralising tendencies, they could have little use for one who wished to revive the *départements* and encourage the use of regional languages. In fact, in pure logic, they could only regard him as a reactionary whose ideas, if put into practice, would necessarily undo most of the work which their ancestors had achieved by the ruthless use of wholesale murder, by the studied use of the basest as well as the cynical misuse of the finest instincts of mankind.

To the tyranny of Empire Mistral indeed opposed the concept of Federalism; but he was too far-sighted ever to be deceived into identifying the cause of Liberty with Benthamite hysteria, anti-clericalism, and political opportunism; and, when he found these things where he sought only justice, he was quick to react—for what is 'reaction' if not a proof that one is more than an automaton?

Mistral was a true revolutionary because he understood the true nature of Liberty: he did not confuse it with licence. The tidal wave of unleashed impulse on the crest of which the French Revolution stormed the beaches of the *ancien régime* has hardened gradually into the wintry icefloes of our contemporary tyrannies. It was natural that Mistral should react against such a development: but it is greatly to his credit that he divined it, for so many have been deceived who unconciously desired, as he did, not a revolution, or even a counter-revolution, but, in the classic phrase of de Maistre, 'the opposite of a revolution'. Perhaps his local patriotism saved him; perhaps his upbringing. But, in the last analysis, political views and philosophical opinions are ultimately reduced to the question of the immortality of the soul, and Mistral answered this question emphatically in the affirmative. Almost every line of his poetry, almost every recorded word that he uttered, exists to prove his passionate belief and delight in Man made in the image of God. Nowhere is he more Mediterranean than in this.

As a political philosopher—and this incarnation of his genius gradually emerges from a study of his life and works—he is, then, poles apart from those with whom he sought to ally himself on that first fruitless journey to Paris; for he is of the company of their bitterest opponents, with Edmund Burke, Donoso Cortés, and Metternich.

Mistral did not, however, abandon politics; he merely abandoned the politicians, and thereafter approached the problem in a different way.

On his return to Provence, in the spring of 1867, he was present at a banquet given by the Irishman, Bonaparte-Wyse, for the Catalans and Provençaux, and was presented by the Catalans with the Coupo Santo, a silver cup 'offered by the Catalan patriots to the Provençal poets in memory of the hospitality shown to the Catalan poet Victor Balaguer'. Mistral replied with a lyric, *La Coupo*, celebrating the event, which begins:

> Men of Provence, behold the cup
> Given us by the Catalans;
> From it, in turn, let us drink up
> The purest vintage of our vines!

The following year the visit was returned, and Mistral, with Bonaparte-Wyse, Louis Roumieux and Paul Meyer, attended the Floral Games at Barcelona; while at Figueras the poet recited his lyric *La Brassado*, celebrating the unity of the two peoples. In the autumn of the same year he wrote to Quintana that if Spain's most devoted and intelligent men would lead her into the path of true liberty by inaugurating a federal régime, they would have the admiration of Europe: an observation of great perspicacity. There were indeed a number of republicans who believed in the federal solution, in the turbulent Spain of that time; but they were in a minority. Mistral was finally to find his ideas most faithfully upheld in a very different quarter.

With a heart warmed in the fire of the purest patriotism, with a judgement unwarped by sentimentality or prejudice, Mistral came at last face to face with the inevitable choice: logic and clear thinking did not permit of compromise or prevarication; honesty demanded that he choose between the Red and the White, between the revolutionaries and the absolutists, between Man-god and God-man. In the autumn of 1872, he wrote to Quintana: 'My soul is at peace'. He had chosen.

In 1871, he wrote a poem round the allegory of Sisyphus which exactly exposes the heart of the matter. For Sisyphus will never succeed in freeing himself from his labour: his pride will not permit it. In vain do the angels implore him to humble himself and repent:

Raising his face, disfigured by derision,
Silent, and disdainful of that white vision,
As do the damned, he looks upon the sky,
And to his labour turns back furiously.

This illusion of liberty, the result of a false interpretation of the meaning of freedom, lies at the root of all our past mistakes and present discontents. For the divine paradox upon which Mistral seized is this: that there is no freedom without authority. He whose pride will not allow him to submit to authority becomes thereby not free, but the abject slave of his own presumption: he has become a Sisyphus, condemned, of his own will, to defiance and frustration. Truly, men are free to become slaves.

It is not surprising therefore that the poet's disillusionment with the revolutionary forces in France was by now complete. In 1870, refusing an official position, he had written: 'Were I to participate in the work of a new Constitution, I would direct all my efforts to ensuring the triumph of the federal principle and I believe, unfortunately, that this idea is not yet understood in France. Our French republicans dream ceaselessly of the benefits of the American and Swiss Constitutions and all, or nearly all, ignore or reject the sole means of attaining them, which is federation.'

To what, then did he turn? He saw clearly, as many have still to see, that, in the words of Marius André: 'There are only two principles in the world: liberty and authority, the republic and the legitimate monarchy', and he wrote: 'All the intermediary régimes, namely: revolutionary monarchies and democratic empires, are only the instruments of dissolution and of corruption. The republic being made fatally impossible in Europe by the frenzy and intolerance of the radicals, there remains only the divine right . . . despite all the declamations and trumpetings of the nineteenth century, the great things of the Latin world have been made by faith and authority. If we do not come back to them by that way, we shall finish like Byzantium.'[1]

These conclusions disturbed his Spanish liberal friends; but, as it happened, events in Spain were to bear him out. In 1870, the Spanish monarchy was restored in the person of a member of the house of Savoy, an unhappy choice and a compromise which, like most compromises, ended unhappily, for two years later Amedeo was forced to abdicate; the republic returned, and with it anarchy.

On the surface, no faction appeared to embody the ideals of the poets; but there was one body, uncompromising, idealistic, and absolutist, which in fact did so. The Carlists of Navarre, who, with the peasants of *La Vendée*, alone in Europe preserve

[1] Quoted from M. André, *Mistral*.

to this day the fervour and faith of the Middle Ages untainted, had, and still have, a creed which is the result of a logical application of Mistral's principles and of the conclusions to which he had come. Offended by their notion of an absolute monarch, most enquirers stop there and go no further. But their concern is basically less with the king than with the kingdom. As their historian, Ramon de Oyarzun, has written: 'The monarchist ideal of the Carlist party is not that of an absolute monarchy, and even less of a despotic or tyrannical one, in which the caprice of the king and his suite is the *suprema lex:* nor of a parliamentary monarchy in which the king reigns without governing—the plaything of factions . . .' Their *suprema lex* was God and the Eternal Law—and did not Mistral write that outside of Christ and the Decalogue there was only 'power, savagery, and dissolution'?—and their king was to be invested with power only to be the social administrator of this law and the guardian of their liberties. For they fought so fanatically not only for their faith, for their king and for their country (*Por Dios, Patria y Re*) but also, it must be remembered, for their *fueros*, that peculiarly Basque institution which asserted the inalienable rights of regional and municipal authority, and was, and in some form must ever be, a part of the essential machinery of federation.

Unlike his Catalan friends, who retained a fear of clericalism and a passion for parliamentary government, Mistral seems to have divined this identity of ends and means, for he wrote, to the dismay of Quintana and Balaguer, whom he attempted to reassure by saying that he wrote not as a politician but as a poet, a poem to the sister-in-law of the Carlist pretender, doña Blanca de Borbon, in which, calling her 'little nightingale of love, singing upon the highest branch' and a 'holy woman who was going out to fight for God against the wicked horde who prevaricate and blaspheme', he says: 'Doña Blanca, lily of Spain, happy is he who . . . makes war with you, happy is he who falls at your feet!' And, in his reply to Quintana's protest, he clearly demonstrates his sympathy for the cause, being heartily sick of the democrats 'who ruin, kill and make a laughing stock of the poor Latin world', and taking delight in the contrast of 'this young princess who mounts her horse and fights in the sun for the tradition of her race and for the religion of her ancestors'; and he ends: 'Poet of the Provençale tradition, son of a language and a nationality that democratic progress would wish to destroy, I am logical in counselling you not to forget that the old Catalans were Catholics and monarchists.'

In fact, many Catalans were Carlist, for Carlism is not merely a movement of Navarre, but a coherent and, indeed, traditional, philosophy of life. In this sense, Carlism was strong in the Provence of that time, for the country people of the Midi largely supported the cause of Henri V, a cause 'Carlist' in all but name;

and of such people, and their leaders, the poet's *entourage* was henceforth largely composed. His friend Scipion Doncieux took up and developed his ideas, as did in our own day another son of the Midi, a great but tragic figure, Charles Maurras.

Marius André tells us that there were a number of these 'Mistralians', at Maillane, Avignon and Montpellier, each of whom possessed 'more French wisdom, logic and foresight than was to be found in the whole Parliament in Paris'; one of whom, the Baron de Tourtoulon, foretells the rise of Germany and the decline of France, in a letter to Mistral's old comrade, Quintana.

This thought with, to Mistral, its clear threat of world war, was to preoccupy him henceforward and lend a special urgency to his advocacy of the federal idea. The association with the Catalans had been prompted by their mutual distaste for the centralization which their respective governments practised so unrepentantly. Now Mistral wished to expand this association until it included the whole Latin world, until he had organised a Latin confederation with which to confront the rising power of Germany. He had, of course, to work without official encouragement or support, for his vision was of that kind which we associate with statesmen and not with politicians: but his efforts were to reveal in him, also, remarkable diplomatic skill.

His first opportunity came in 1874, the fifth centenary of the death of Petrarch, and he seized it eagerly. With Doncieux, Roger du Demaine, Aubanel and Roumanille he organised a festival to take place, appropriately enough, at Avignon. Despite opposition from the governments concerned, notably France and Italy, and the attempts of the republicans and democrats to steal the thunder for themselves (they hailed Petrarch as the precursor of Garibaldi) the ceremony was a complete success and a triumph for Mistral and his associates, that band of reactionary clericals, traditionalists and poets which its opponents sought so earnestly and so ineffectively to discredit. The whole affair was in fact a diplomatic *coup* that put to shame and exposed the policies of the governments concerned, which, as events were to prove, served only to prepare their countries, and Europe, for her ultimate dissolution. These governments, who practised imperialism in the name of national security and licence in the name of liberty were, however, in power; and though they might be shaken, could not be removed from the eminence in which they were secured by the mobocracy they had introduced and the skill in deception in which, to our detriment, they were continually to improve.

Their success led the 'Mistralians' to a further effort. A second opportunity presented itself with the advent of the Floral Games, organised by the *Société des langues romanes*, which were to be held the following year at the old university city of Montpellier. In the nature of things this occasion could hardly carry the implications or have the repercussions of the earlier event at Avignon: but the question of a Latin federation was introduced by a message from Professor Ascoli, of Milan, which was read out at the Games, and the occasion was memorable for a remarkable speech delivered by Mistral himself which admirably expresses the breadth, splendour and warmth of his vision, and which, at the same time, serves to refute those who impute, or imputed, separatist aims to the 'Mistralians':

> ... France, as you know, has not always hung her head over her grieving heart; France, our mother, was once the queen of nations in the arts of peace and in those of war. But, then, people lived more naturally, and nobody was ashamed to speak like his mother, and nobody blushed for his village and, in order to love France, it was not necessary to affect French. For, whether one were called the chevalier d'Assas or the drummer of Arcola, when one had to go, one went; when one had to die, one died.
> ... Do not let us forget, love of country is not the result of opinion, or decree, or fashion. Great patriotism is born of a man's attachment to his country, to his customs, to his family; and the best soldiers, believe me, are not those who sing and who cry when they have drunk; they are those who weep when they leave their homes.
> Consequently, gentlemen, if we wish to restore our poor country, let us restore that which breeds patriots: religion, traditions, national memories, the old language of the country; and, city by city, province by province, let us compete in study, work and honour, to exalt in different ways the name of France ...[1]

Further impetus to the movement was given by Quintana's offer, which was accepted, of a prize for the best poem on the Latin race, to be awarded at the next concourse. This third, and greater, occasion took place in May, 1878, at Montpellier, and was successful despite ever-increasing opposition. In a speech at the Ste-Estelle banquet Mistral had likened the work of the Felibres to the apostolic mission of the apostles after they had received the gift of tongues at Pentecost. His opponents saw it—or pretended to see it—as disruptive, subversive and separatist: it was a case of assault by misrepresentation, which, though it failed to pervert the nature and the purpose of the concourse at Montpellier, did the movement as a whole great harm.

The Floral Games, brilliantly organised by Tourtoulon, lasted seven days, included shooting and musical contests and games, and were lavishly attended. The main event, the poetic prize,

---

[1] Quoted from M. André, op. cit.

was won by the Roumanian, Vasili Alecsandri, a judgement influenced, beyond doubt, by diplomatic as much as aesthetic considerations; for Mistral himself submitted a poem, one of the best known and by no means the least of his lyrics, which could hardly be bettered in its kind. Alecsandri's poem is, however, not without fervour, and ends: 'At the day of judgement, when in heaven, face to face with the Lord God, the Latin race is asked: 'What have you done on this earth?' she will reply, firmly 'O! Lord God, while I was in the world . . . I represented you!'

Mistral's *Cant a la raço latino* is at once more subtle and more profound: in fact, it is a sublimation of his patriotic beliefs and aspirations:

> Arise, arise, O Latin race,
> Beneath the great cope of the Sun!
> The Lord's wine gushes from the press,
> The dark grape bubbles in the tun.
>
> Your hair unbound upon the wind
> That blows from Tabor's sacred height,
> Yours is the clarity of mind
> That lives on joy and on delight;
> You are the Apostolic race
> That rings the bells across the plain;
> The silver trumpeter of Grace;
> The hand that sows the golden grain.
>
> Your mother tongue, that mighty stream
> Which seven arteries supplies,
> Whose flood of love and flame must seem
> An echo out of Paradise,
> Your golden tongue (Rome's daughter too!)
> Is that great song that will be heard
> On every human lip anew
> While there is meaning in the Word.
>
> * * *
>
> Upon your sun-soaked slopes there grows
> The olive-tree, the staff of peace;
> And through your countryside there blows
> The swelling vine, in proud increase:
> So let your past, O Latin race,
> Your fate upon your heart emboss;
> Arise, salute the morning's face,
> One Brotherhood beneath the Cross!

VI

This poem appears in one of Mistral's two collections of lyric poems, *Lis Isclo d'Or* (*The Isles of Gold* or *Les Iles d'Hyères*) which, first published by Roumanille at Avignon in 1875, appeared in a second edition, revised and corrected, in 1878. He had married Mlle Marie-Louise Rivière, of whom he wrote: 'I have found at last . . . the incarnation of that which I sought in Mirèio and Esterello', and again: 'She is charming, beautiful, and with a passion for great and heroic things.' It was the marriage of 'genius with beauty', wrote Aubanel. An altogether happy union, it added a tender theme to the harmonious symphony of his life.

Lis Isclo d'Or is divided into sections, songs, romances, *serventés*, 'dreams', *plaintes*, sonnets, nuptial songs, and salutations, interspersed with longer poems, such as *Lou Tambour d'Arcolo* (*The Drummer of Arcola*) and *La Fin dóu Meissounié* (*The Passing of the Reaper*). It begins appropriately enough with a hymn to the sun, *Lou Cant dóu Soulèu*, that sun which brings life and joy to Provence:

> Great sun that shines upon Provence,
> And the mistral's gay companion,
> You who can stagger the Durance,
> Like a wave of the Crau wine,
>
> Let your fair lamp blaze brilliantly!
> Hunt shadow and catastrophe!
>   Quickly! quickly! quickly!
> Let us now your radiance see!

and the first section, *Li Cansoun*, the songs, includes *La Coupo*, to which we have already referred, and *Lis Enfant d'Ourfiéu* (*The Children of Orpheus*) a reference to their Greek ancestors, with its lovely refrain:

> Let us sing our father's glory
>   That in story
>   Is renowned,
> They who ever, in our history
>   Have been free
> As the ocean and the wind.

All these songs are clear, straightforward, objective, shapely, and show that fondness for diverse stanza-forms and rhyme-schemes characteristic of their author.

Lou Tambour d'Arcolo which follows is a longer piece celebrating an episode in the progress of the army in Italy under Buonaparte: it is a patriotic ballad of great speed and energy.

The Romances, on the other hand, refer to the more fanciful episodes of Provençal history and legend, and tell their stories musically, effortlessly, and with great variety. Many call to mind, in manner as in matter, the songs of the Troubadours. *L'Amiradou* begins: 'Au castèu de Tarascoun i'a 'no rèino, i'a 'no fado', ('In the castle of Tarascon lives a queen, a fairy'); *Lou Renegat* tells of one captured by corsairs, and *Catelan lou Troubaire* is set in the time of *la bello Margarido*, who lived for love.

The second long poem, really an extended Romance, *La Princesso Clemènço*, tells of a Princess who was as 'beautiful as the sea is huge' and begins with the traditional directness of popular poetry:

> Once upon a time we had in our Provence
> A king called Charles the Second, who was lame.

and the story unfolds with a matter-of-fact elegance.

There follows the collection of *Serventés*, which includes an ode to the Catalan poets, an elegy for Jasmin, who 'sang of love better than a woman', the ode to the Latin race, the poem on the legend of Sisyphus, and, not least, the remarkable *Penitential Psalm*, inspired by the war of 1870, in which Mistral asks God's pardon for the sins and follies of his race that brought down this vengeance on their heads:

> Lord God, we have turned our backs
> On thy commandments
> And thy sacraments,
> Brutes, our faith all substance lacks,
> Who live for selfishness
> And trust in Progress!

This poem, which is long, has a sombre colouring rare in Mistral.

Li Serventés are divided from *Li Pantai (Dreams)* by *La Fin dóu Meissounié*, a superb fresco, with all the statuesque quality of the finest scenes in *Mirèio*. The scene has the immobility of a frieze, the gestures of its figures the timeless beauty of actions performed in the morning of the world.

> On the rough hurdle the old harvester
> Was lying, drenched with blood and very pale,
> And raising his bare arm bronzed by sun and gale,
> Spoke thus to the reapers there.

As the poem opens, however, the old harvester is speaking: 'Gather the ears of corn', he says, 'and don't worry about me . . . don't leave it to the mice and the birds, the corn that comes from God': and, standing round about him, their sickles in their hands, the other harvesters listen, while the women cry out and the children cling to their mothers. Then we are told how the accident happened. Under a blazing sun, which 'boiled the blood in one's veins', the old man was leading the younger harvesters through the cornfield, hacking a way through at furious speed. It is too much for the old man. For the first time he feels the effects of age, trembles, and hesitates: but, behind him, the younger men sweep on, 'like the waves of the sea', and one of them wounds the leader mortally, with a great blow from his sickle. Then the second stanza, already quoted, is repeated, and we are once more listening to the words of the dying man. This arrangement of the time-element in the poem, or rearrangement of the sequence, is characteristic and enhances still further the effect of timelessness already made by the serene movement of the verse.

The harvester pleads with them not to weep; it would be better to sing with the young people, although

> . . . in the land where I am soon to be,
> When evening comes, it may seem sad, no more
> Stretched out upon the pasture as before
> To hear fair youth's strong, limpid melody
>   Between the branches soar.

Yet it is fate, or perhaps God on high who, seeing that the corn is ripe, has come to harvest it. Then, after an interval, being thirsty, the old man drinks a little cold water, replaces the pitcher on the golden corn, and fixes his eyes upon the setting sun.

> And suddenly he raised his arms on high,
> His eyes were luminous with mystery:
> 'St John of summer, lord St John', cried he,
> 'Patron of reapers, father of the poor,
> Now in your Paradise remember me!'

And he asks St John to remember his olive-yard, and his family, whom he leaves behind in the mountains and who, at Christmas, must sup without him; and he asks forgiveness if he has complained of his lot, but 'even the sickle cries out when it meets a stone': and the scene closes as serenely and as statuesquely as it began.

> And the old man was dead: his sight effaced,
> But like white marble had his body flowered;
> Sickle in hand the reapers in hushed haste
>   Back to their labour raced
> For a mistral of flame the corn devoured.

37

There follow the 'dreams', the first of which, *La Coumunioun di Sant*, has a religious setting. The second *Romanin* is an evocation of the past. In *Lou Prègo-Diéu* (*The Praying Mantis*) the poet builds round the contemplation of an insect an unexpectedly melancholy meditation: 'flesh is lovely, and decays, the wave is bitter and I would drink, full of languor, I want to die–and live'. *Lou Blad de Luno* (*The Lunar Corn*)–which is the title of a book of poems by a great Provençal poet and *gardian* of this century, the Marquis of Baroncelli-Javon–is an eerie and romantic poem with an hypnotic refrain. *Lou Lioun d'Arle* (*The Lion of Arles*) which follows, describes a climb to a peak in the Alpilles, shaped in the form of a lion, whither the poet has gone to seek, as from an oracle, the revelation of the destiny of Provence.

Li Plang (*The Complaints*) are, as the name implies, of a more intimate nature: in these poems Mistral rivals Aubanel, a specialist, in the expression of amorous moods, veiled by a pure melancholy: they bear such titles as Meeting, Incandescence, Discouragement, Ennui, Languor, Rancour; and among them is a beautiful poem to the *felibresso*, Antonnieto de Beu-Caire, who died young; it ends with the verse:

> You pierce for us the holy mist
> That hides the light of loftiest
> Intellect supernal:
> And now great marvels are your common theme
> And none shall wake you from your golden dream
> For you possess in full the truth eternal.

As if there were not already enough variety, richness and splendour in this book, *Lis Isclo d'Or* contains also the *Sonnets;* the *Nuptial Songs*, written mostly for members of the Felibrige, for Aubanel, for Félix Gras, for La felibresso Bremoundo; and the *Salutations*, to such as Lamartine and Gounod, which include *La Brassado*, the poem written for the Catalans, to which we have already referred. The diversity of subject matter, feeling, treatment and technical resource of this collection is indeed extraordinary, and the whole, the more if we consider it in relation to Mistral's other works and activities, exhibits that many-sided richness which is one of the hallmarks of greatness.

VII

Among the *Sonnets* in *Lis Isclo d'Or* is one, *Au Miejour* (*To the Midi*), which was inscribed at the head of the *Tresor dóu Felibrige*, a vast dictionary of the dialects of the Midi upon which Mistral had been working ever since that first visit to Paris, and which began to appear, in yearly instalments, from 1878. In the sonnet, the poet describes how the plough may turn up a Roman bronze, which shines in the sun amid the rising corn. He asks the people of the Midi to dip into his treasury in the same way, in order to 'reconquer the empire of your language'.

While following him in his political and patriotic activities we have seen something of the importance the poet attached to language. He regarded it, indeed, as the 'master-root of all patriotism, the powerful leaven of all freedom'[1], and these words gain weight if we recall that the decline of Austria-Hungary, the sole heir of nothing less than the Holy Roman Empire, really began when the otherwise enlightened Emperor, Joseph II, decreed German as the official language of all its member states. That the compilation of this dictionary, an exhausting and pioneer labour, was no mere scholastic exercise but rather, in its author's eyes, a patriotic duty, may be inferred from this eloquent extract of a speech delivered at the Ste-Estelle banquet, in 1877:

A language is like the shaft of a mine for at the bottom of it there have been deposited all the fears, all the feelings, all the thoughts, of ten, twenty, thirty, a hundred generations. It is a pile, an ancient hoard, whither every passer-by has brought his gold or silver or leather coin. It is a great monument whither every family has carried its stone, where every city has built its column, where a whole race has worked, body and soul, for hundreds and thousands of years. A language, in a word, is the revelation of actual life, the manifestation of human thought, the all-holy instrument of civilizations, and the speaking testament of dead and living societies.[1]

The thoroughness with which Mistral was wont to pursue his philological studies may be seen in the notes to *Calendau;* in the names of the fish enumerated by the hero; in the tracing of place-names; in the listing of synonyms and derivations, from the Greek, for example, as with *bletoun*, a nail, βλῆτρον; *broufounié*, the noise of a tempest, βαρυφωνία; or *gàngui*, a net, γαγγάρη; or in the noting of local variants as with the word for the marge of a river: in the dialect of Toulon, *la margo;* Romance, *marca;* Latin, *margo;* but in the mouths of 'les messieurs', *la malgue*.

It was a giant task, but it was successfully accomplished. The Treasury earned not merely the gratitude of Mistral's followers, but the approval of the philologists: in 1890, it was awarded the Grand Prix de l'Académie des Inscriptions et Belles-Lettres and Bruno Durand, keeper of the Library at Aix-en-Provence, described it as a 'Triple mystery of love, of patriotism, and of genius'.[2]

---

1 Quoted from C. M. Girdlestone, *Dreamer and Striver* (London, Methuen, 1937) p. 161.
2 Quoted from Paul Souchon, *Mistral*, p. 156.

Lou Tresor dóu Felibrige was completed in 1878, and in that same year Mistral published another long poem, *Nerto*, slighter in matter and in manner than the two preceding, and rather an historical narrative than an epic. In the place of the original stanza which he had previously employed, the poet turned for this fanciful piece to rhymed octosyllabic couplets. Full of delightful poetry, it is not, however, central to its author's thought; and, pointing no patriotic moral, is content to adorn an historical tale.

In his memoirs, Mistral tells how it is founded on a legend told to him by a peasant. The story is of a girl, Nerto, whose soul has been vowed to the Devil by her father. Learning of this on her father's death, Nerto journeys to Avignon to implore the aid of the Pope, Benedict XIII. At this point there is woven into the story the thread of an historical counter-subject (to borrow a musical term) built round the events at Avignon brought about by the Schism of Western Christendom. Nerto arrives during the siege and, once inside the Palace, meets Roudrigo, the Pope's nephew, who falls in love with her. The episode is preceded by a description of the City of Avignon in the great days of its splendour, when its streets were thronged with cardinals, soldiers, sailors, ambassadors and scholars.

Nerto at last obtains an audience and is received by the Pope as one sent by God; meanwhile the siege has intensified and the towers of the great palace are burning. In a scene of great magnificence Benedict XIII appears to the people and bestows upon them the papal blessing, *urbi et orbi*. Then this last Pope to reign in Avignon disappears into the shade 'like the sun at the close of day'. Mistral superbly evokes this tragic figure against a tumultuous background, in verse that is not uncoloured by patriotic as well as religious fervour, and indeed, according to Baroncelli-Javon, he was of the view that the balance of Christendom would have been better preserved had the Papacy remained at Avignon.

These events occupy the second canto. The third is dominated by the figure of Louis, King of Anjou and Count of Provence, who comes with his court to Château-Renard to seek the papal blessing upon his marriage, shortly to be celebrated at Arles. The marriage, at St Trophime, is described in the canto that follows, as are the fights in the arena and the celebrations which accompany it. Nerto, meanwhile, has entered a convent, on the Pope's advice: in the fifth canto, she takes the veil in the presence of Pope, King, and Queen. A pathetic passage describes the inevitable sacrifice of her beautiful hair. Nerto is an unwilling aspirant: but Roudrigo breaks into the convent and carries her off. Attacked in the process, he is forced to abandon her, at night, in the open country.

The scene changes to the rocky Alpilles, whither she has

wandered and where she meets a hermit whose food is brought
to him by an angel. The atmosphere of this canto is pure, rarefied
and luminous; a thing of clear, bright air, and distant, tinkling
bells; it discovers, in contrast to the pomp and clamour of
Avignon, the lonely faith of the solitary, of a visual simplicity:

> Down below, the world is white;
> And overhead, the world is light.
> And on the summit of the hill,
> In his hood, so rapt and still,
> The hermit is in ecstasy.
> It is as if life passed him by
> And the spirit watched alone.
> The Angel speaks, observed by none,
> But the hermit's pupils quail
> To see his wings arise and pale,
> To mingle with the azure steep
> Of space, so luminous and deep,
> And tremble like a distant sail.

Through the angel's intervention the old man is forced to send
Nerto back to her convent. She is intercepted by a device of the
Devil's, an enchanted castle built at Roudrigo's request. There
they meet and, faced with the purity and sweetness of Nerto's
person and speech, her lover repents of his past actions so that
when the Devil appears to claim his due, Roudrigo is able to
invert his sword, and holding up the pommelled cross, to cry
out: 'In the name of the Father, Son, and Holy Ghost, get thee
behind me!' The castle disappears in a sheet of flame and an
epilogue shows us Nerto and Roudrigo entering Paradise.

This legendary and fantastic poem is most notable for its
beautiful descriptions, the living warmth of its leading figures,
Nerto, Roudrigo, the Pope and the King, and for its glorification
of the Avignonese Papacy. The most strikingly religious of
Mistral's works, it received the apostolic blessing of Pius X,
in 1910.

VIII

In the year that *Nerto* appeared, Mistral went to Paris to attend
the Ste Estelle banquet in honour of the union between Provence and France. The atmosphere was much changed. The
hostility which his earlier efforts had aroused had evaporated;
he was welcomed as a great poet and the head of a large and
influential movement. He was assured of election to the Acad-
emy, but chose to decline the honour. And once again, at the
banquet, he reiterated his fundamental principles:

For four hundred years the States General of Provence has been saying to France: 'The country of Provence, with its azure sea, its Alps and its plains, of its own free will is united with thee, O France! not as an accessory to a principal, but as one principal to another, which is to say that we will keep our liberties, our customs, and our language . . .' It is in the Provençale tongue that the conscript from the banks of the Rhône, that the drummer of Arcola cried his last cry on the field of battle; and if our deputies and senators are silent and forgetful, we poets, representatives of the people by the grace of God, with our poems which will resound in the very heart of Paris, will protest for ever . . . France is great; from the vast Ocean to the Latin sea, from the Sahara to Tonkin, a hundred peoples live free beneath the folds of her flag. Some have the sun, with the olive and the pomegranate that hang in the sky; others the freshness, the verdant meadows where the cattle graze; here they sing the sea and there the mountains; and sacred nature has given to all the aptitudes and the language which they need for their growth . . . O France, mother France, leave then to thy Provence, to thy delightful Midi, the melodious language in which she says to you: My mother!. . .[1]

On his return from Paris, Mistral turned to the drama. The dramatic literature of Provence was of the slightest: almost the only great play it possessed was Aubanel's *Lou Pan dóu Pecat* (*The Bread of Sin*), savage, violent and sombre. Undoubtedly, Mistral planned to write a national drama, as he had written a national epic.

La Rèino Jano, which appeared in 1890, is a tragedy in five acts: the time is the fourteenth century, when Queen Joan of Naples and Countess of Provence and of Anjou married, at the age of fifteen, Andrew of Hungary. The first three acts are laid in Naples, and culminate in the assassination of Andrew, a crime of which the Queen is accused. She journeys to Avignon to plead her innocence before the Pope. Her voyage to Marseilles occupies the fourth act; while the fifth brings before us her trial and eventual acquittal.

We have never seen this play performed and a majority of critics judges it a failure as a stage-drama. It is not undramatic, and there is action and suspense; the plot is coherent, and the poet has not fallen into the usual error of poets who sacrifice the drama to the verse; but it is architecturally weak. Mistral himself confirmed, or anticipated, the general verdict in a letter written two years after the play's appearance in which he remarked that he doubted if it would take kindly to the boards, that the drama was not his *métier*, but that the tragedy might make an effective libretto for an opera.

[1] Quoted from M. André, op. cit. p. 198-9.

The conventions of opera, however, demand concentration: only the last two acts might make effective operatic scenes. The fourth act indeed is already music, while the fifth is crowded with choruses. Probably it would be best performed as an historical pageant, in a stylised production, and if possible in the open air; in, say, the ancient amphitheatre of Arles where today, under the bowl of a starry summer night, Greek tragedies are played. It would then have the space which its episodes demand, and the perfect setting for its poetry.

About one thing, however, there can be no question: in his heroine Mistral has created one of his most vital characters. True, his patriotism triumphs over his historical judgement, and his Queen is relieved of the character bestowed upon her by proverbially unerring Time; but this is of no consequence, for his Jano is rather an incarnation of Provence than a reincarnation of that fourteenth century Queen of Naples who was so cruel, so amorous, and so compelling.

Here she is rather the triumph of Life over Death, indulging her passionate individuality with the gay abandon of those figures in the Decameron whose hungry comedies are played against the grim background of the Black Death. There is no aphrodisiac like abstinence, and life is never so hectic as when it must assert itself in the midst of cruelty, suffering, and danger. The silken pomp with which such a life was clothed had but to be torn to reveal barbaric passions: no wonder there was need of custom and ritual! The finest flowers of Italian art blossomed amid the bloody feuds, the perpetual conflicts, of the Renaissance; and Provence herself discovered the immortal gaiety of her spirit against a background of horror. In Jano she seems to speak with the mingled clamour of her mixed and volatile blood, and to speak in an historical and yet timeless incarnation in a manner and with a force impossible in the pastoral world which is Mirèio's.

One critic has seen in the restless, undefined ambition of this character a reflection of the modern woman, the displaced product of a society whose foundations are disintegrating. But, in fact, women of this commanding type, in which every passion and every faculty are developed with a truly feminine intensity, are the products, not of our sentimental, biologically unsound emancipation—as it is called—but of a society which allows them to develop to their fullest extent *as women*.

Jano is no suffragette, although impatient of all convention, in this resembling another wild and tragic spirit, Elizabeth of Austria: and, whereas Elizabeth found the elusive symbol of her freedom in the horses and wide plains of her native Hungary, Jano finds hers in the sea. In the fourth act, on her way to Marseilles, she is seated on deck under a golden awning; she watches the white sail shining against the dark blue sky, and

43

admires the beautiful motion of the half-naked oarsmen; and she is flooded by that sense of incompleteness which comes to passionate natures when, in moments of repose and contemplation, they feel, chafing at their souls, the chains of a finite existence:

O that in light I were dissolved away!
In veiléd sense of God's infinity
I faint . . . In love, and lovely, is the sea,
A happy queen, pellucid in her glory!

'La mar es uno encantarello', 'the sea is an enchantress', she exclaims, and she is enchanted.

Finally, this royal incarnation of the passionate but elusive soul of Provence is also the symbol of the poet's patriarchal conception of government. She loves her subjects and would be loved by them; her rule would be a personal rule for she is as impatient of the machinery of government as she is of the mechanism of social convention. Standing forth as the projection of her country and the image of its nature and its aspirations, as only the product of a monarchical institution can do, she would enter into that personal relationship with her people, collectively and individually, which only the divine right can regularly afford; would confine within the comprehensible limits of a human personality all the character and all the history of her race; bearing the past in her soul, the present in her heart, and the future in her head.

If, therefore, La Rèino Jano is to be counted a failure as a stage play, this must not blind us to its qualities; to its historical magnificence; to its inspiring example; to the profound insight which it provides into Mistral's deepest longings, thus holding up as it were a mirror to his country's soul; and last but not least, to the great poetry which lends it wings, celebrating the sea with the same fervour as went to celebrate the countryside in Mirèio.

IX

The author of La Rèino Jano had long felt the need to maintain a closer, more immediate and more regular contact with his people than had hitherto been possible through the medium of his poems, his convocations, his speeches, or the Armana, a Provençal anthology which appeared at yearly intervals; and in 1891 there appeared the first number of L'Aioli, a paper designed to 'renew the heart of Provence', which was to appear three times a month for nine years, and which aimed to appeal to a wider circle of readers than had been solicited before. L'Aioli (its title is taken from the name of a popular Provençal sauce, compounded of mayonnaise and garlic) was directed by Folco, Marquis of Baroncelli-Javon, then a very young man and one of Mistral's most ardent disciples, who was later to become a fine lyric poet in his own right and who would in his turn be succeeded by his nephew Joseph d'Arbaud.

The first number of *L'Aioli* was something of an event, and, as was only right, its front page carried a manifesto written by Mistral himself, but signed 'The Editors'. 'L'aioli', he wrote, explaining the title, 'in its essence, concentrates the heat, the strength, the gaiety of the sun of Provence . . . We, the good Provençaux . . . will vote for the oil and will make aioli, that is to say, liaison, rally, union:' and he goes on to assert that their ultimate aim is federation, in terms with which we are already familiar.

Mistral worked at *L'Aioli* with the same care which he gave to his poems and, indeed, to everything that he did. Despite its founders' immense prestige, its path, however, was not altogether smooth. The members of the Felibrige, united on the main purpose of that institution, which was the preservation of the Langue d'Oc, were by no means unanimous over the question of federation, for there were among their number republicans and anticlericals like Felix Gras, as well as the wholehearted 'Mistralians'. *L'Aioli* for its part was rather the organ of what Mistral called the 'federal youth'; it gathered round its standard the young and energetic, the best poets and the best brains, who ventured forth to battle blessed by the apostle of their movement, Father Xavier de Fourvières.

The conflict came to a head when, at a banquet given at Paris in honour of Félix Gras in 1892, Frédéric Amouretti rose and read out the 'Declaration of the young Felibres', composed by himself and Charles Maurras, both ardent Mistralians. It contained such statements as:

> Before everything, we reclaim the freedom of our *communes;* we wish them to become mistresses of their essential functions and of their functionaries. We wish that they might put in their place these fine gentlemen called sub-prefects . . . We would deliver from their departmental cages the souls of the provinces whose beautiful names are still borne everywhere by all, Gascons, Auvergnats, Limousins, Béarnais, Dauphinois, Roussillonnais, Provençaux and Languedociens . . . We are autonomists, we are federalists . . . we would have a sovereign assembly at Bordeaux, Toulouse, Montpellier; we would have one at Marseilles or at Aix . . . We are drunk neither with words nor phrases. We are moved by a profound feeling for the national interest. We await, of course, the intellectual and moral renaissance of the Midi, but we desire something more: the complete fulfilment of the riches of our soil . . . We are not

45

the first in this hope. The masterpieces of Mistral are full of this idea . . .

This 'Carlist' declaration stunned the company; and the Jacobins rallied to the assault. Unable, or unwilling, to attack Mistral himself, whose position was by now virtually unassailable to the extent that any attack upon the poet personally would rebound upon his assailant, they directed their fire against the 'federal youth'. Mistral in fact knew nothing of this declaration and it came as a surprise to him: it was, however, a welcome surprise, and he reprinted the text on the front page of *L'Aioli* with a note of endorsement, thus frustrating at one stroke his opponents' counter-attack. Though Maurras and Amouretti were expelled from the Parisian Felibrige, the group which formed round them rapidly established itself and, with Mistral's warm approbation and encouragement, went from strength to strength.

L'Aioli came to an end in 1898; but its work was done. It had led and trained a generation who were now able to carry on the cause in the wider fields of the established press, in Paris and in the provinces. It was Mistral's last polemical work; thereafter he could relinquish his hold on events, could hand over to the young poets and leaders who having looked to him for inspiration had grown to intellectual maturity under his patriarchal care.

At this point it is appropriate to consider the results of Mistral's intense labours as a Felibrige, a patriot, and a federalist.

Among the most attractive and most gifted of Mistral's admirers was a follower of Maurras, Léon Daudet. He knew the poet and, in his memoirs, gives an excellent picture of the man and summary of his work:

> Those who met the principal members of this group had the privilege of knowing collaborators in a great work, the preservation of contact between a race and its traditions. Opposing the Jacobins and the levelling processes of democracy, hostile to the ugliness of false 'realism', these inspired poets, while labouring on behalf of one small district, helped to strengthen the nation as a whole. Fifty years passed before their noble work was entirely understood, before its conservative tendencies became apparent . . .
>
> . . . What one notices particularly in Mistral's remarks are their depth, the symmetry of his point of view, the broadness of his vision, as befits a descendant of men who have looked long on wide fields and star-filled skies. So I remember him down the vista of thirty years or more, judging equitably men and events, singing the praises of his province, and elaborating methodically, unremittingly his idea for her reconstruction, on a scale more grand than even his friends have realized . . . In

46

Paris, Mistral was criticized . . . Since then it has been proved that Mistral's ideas were anything but chimeric, that they were sternly practical. The attitude of the Master of Maillane stimulated and encouraged the superb resistance of Alsace and Lorraine; those who upheld the heroic soul of Alsace, her hopes and customs, did so with the weapons that Mistral had forged . . . Incomparably the most gifted of all our poets—including Hugo—Frédéric Mistral is familiar with those formulas that link the State and the Word and add to the strength of both . . . Those shelters which he constructed and of which he sang will, in days to come, afford a refuge for defeated nations seeking to escape the yoke of their oppressors.

This was written in 1913, a year before the poet's death. Since then, events have not sustained the hopes which the future held out to his followers.

But the disasters which we have survived and the greater disasters which threaten us do not invalidate either Mistral's work, or his ideas. On the contrary, they serve merely to throw a poignant light upon their profundity and set the truth of their begetter's conclusions upon a more dazzling eminence.

X

Mistral's rich nature was able to function at several levels simultaneously and, in the midst of these various activities he had been composing another epic. His first, *Mirèio*, is the poem of the countryside, of the farms and the plains; the second, *Calendau*, sings the mountains and the sea; while the last, *Lou Pouèmo dóu Rose*, is the poem of a great river, the Rhône.

In contrast to its predecessors it is composed in unrhymed decasyllables, divided into *laisses* like the *Chanson de Roland*, and recalling the early poem, *Li Meissoun*. It describes the journey of a barge down the river in the days of horse navigation, and this theme, which is treated with a greater realism than the poet had ever previously employed, is combined with another of the highest fantasy, involving two characters, the one legendary, the other unearthly. But the real hero is the mighty river itself, and the very lines seem, as one reads, to reflect the various moods of the undulating and ever-moving waters. *Lou Pouèmo dóu Rose*, unlike the other poems, begins without ceremony:

> They are leaving Lyons at first light,
> The watermen who rule over the Rhône.
> These Condrillots are mighty-muscled men,
> Light-hearted, lusty, and a race who stand
> Ever bolt-upright on their rafts of fir,

47

Their faces gilded to the hue of bronze
By the sun's heat and by the river's glare.
But then, I tell you, more than ever now,
Was seen that kind of heavy-bearded giant,
Huge, bulky, powerful, like a forest oak,
Could lift a beam as though it were a straw—
From poop to prow they bellowed and they swore
Both loud and long, to warm each other's hearts,
From their great vats deep-swilling the red wine down
And from the pot drawing juicy hunks of meat.
There was a fine din all the river's length,
From north to south, without a break or pause,
'Turn her downstream now, ho! Royaume! Empire![1]
Prow upstream! On, now! Pull on the tow-ropes!'

The lives and homes of the boatmen are described in this straightforward way, until suddenly the poet falls into a vein of reverie, lamenting the passing of this open and vigorous life:

O the old times, so simple and so gay,
When all life seemed to bubble on the Rhône
When we came down as children to see pass
The proud Condrillots, on the broad water,
Hands to the tiller! Then the Rhône, thanks to them,
Was a huge beehive, full of noise and work.
Today, all that is silence, huge and dead,
Alas! and of that movement all that's left
Is but a trace, and the corroded furrow
That some old cable rubbed into the stone.

There follows a description of the various barges, including the *Caburle*, which is to play a leading part in the poem: its master is Apian, a typical Mistralian patriarch:

Patron Apian himself upon the poop
Directs the operations from the rail.
He has long hair that hangs in grey locks braided
And round about his temples curls and falls,
And two big, golden rings that are suspended
Down from his ears. And he is tall of stature
And his bright eyes dwell now upon each boat
To see that all goes well and is in order
As one after another, linked in file
By the long cable that holds them all together,
Clearing the shore amid the gurgling water,
All now in line, the barges sail away.

1 The old names for the banks of the river.

and, at length, the long convoy of barges sets sail for Beaucaire, as Apian recites the Lord's Prayer.

The theme of fantasy is introduced in the second canto, with the appearance of Guihén, Prince d'Aurenjo, or William, Prince of Orange and son of the King of Holland, who boards the boat at Vernaison. Young, fair, and almost spectral, he has about him a quality of dreamy romanticism which recalls Troubadours like Rudel. He has set out to seek his ideal under the symbol of the *Zwanenbloem*, or swan's flower of his own country, and the mention of it introduces a reference to the 'heroine', *L'Angloro*, a mysterious figure, the Undine of de la Motte Fouqué, the Ondine of Ravel:

> . . . that is the 'flower of the Rhône', my good prince,
> The flowering rush that grows beneath the wave
> And which L'Angloro loves so much to pluck!

The rest of the canto is concerned with the arrival at and departure from Condrieu, where the boatmen meet their families, and with those easy and natural conversations of which Mistral is a master and which serve him on the one hand for exposition and on the other to describe the habits and customs of the watermen and the technicalities of their trade. So, starkly contrasted, realism and dream alternate in the gently flowing and flexible verse through the third canto and the fourth, in which the barge takes on three Venetian women who go to the great fair at Beaucaire to practise that calling for which the ladies of Venice are so justly famous. One of their number sings a ballad which evokes in the Prince a memory of the barcarolles that, sung in the summer evening, drift up from the waters of the Grand Canal: they were no doubt in Mistral's mind too, for he had visited Venice, with his wife, in the year that *L'Aioli* first appeared and while there had heard, to his great grief, of the death of Roumanille.

The leisurely movement of the poem grows more tense in the fifth canto with the appearance of L'Angloro. In this character the two themes, the realistic and the fantastic, meet and merge: for, when the barge arrives at the point where the Ardèche joins the Rhône, she is standing there on the shore, and turns out to be a gold-washer, who with her precarious gains helps to support her father. This simple and even humble person lives upon two levels, the matter-of-fact and the legendary, for she is the vehicle for the poet's immaterial reverie. Much courted by the watermen, she will have none of them and seems to prefer her lonely independence. There is much good-natured back-chat between her and the crew and it is not until the sixth canto that we see the other side of her nature: for this peasant girl is a child of the river and her mind is filled with dreams and visions of its mys-

49

terious divinity, *Lou Dra*, a kind of protean dragon, a green
serpent who lures mortal women down beneath the waves to his
watery home. Had she not herself seen him, and felt him, one
summer night when she went swimming in the river?

The whole scene is a masterpiece of description and sugges-
tion, which is broken off abruptly as the seventh canto begins and
we return to the train of barges. It has reached Malatra where
L'Angloro comes on board with her father, and the moment she
sees the Prince she reacts with the classic swiftness of the romantic
character who meets with her predestined lover. Pale and
trembling,

> 'It's he! It's he!' she cried like one gone mad

and Guihèn replies:

> I recognize thee,
> Flower of the Rhône that blooms upon the wave!
> Flower of delight half-glimpsed as in a dream . . .

and decisively she answers him:

> 'I recognize thee, O Dra! whom I have seen
> With that same flowering rush beneath the water . . .

Guihèn gives her the flower, and their fate is sealed:

> For love grows fast,
> Once they are in the boat that bears them on,
> Foredoomed, upon the wave.

Meanwhile the convoy moves on its way down-stream:

> The arcades
> Of the Pont St Esprit, with splendid sweep,
> Passed by in soaring triumph overhead . . .
> . . . Provence appeared; for she is heralded
> By the Pont St Esprit with its vast piles,
> Its twenty royal arches that are set
> Like a great coronet upon the Rhône.
> This is the holy and triumphant gate
> Of the land of love! And the olive trees,
> And the pomegranate, proudly flowering,
> And the millet with its abundant hair
> Already deck the marges and the banks.
> The plain spreads out, the verge grows ever greener,
> And in the limpid, paradisal air,
> Are seen the northern slopes of Mont Ventour . . .

The legendary atmosphere returns and is maintained as L'Angloro tells the company of the oracle at the fountain of Tourne, where there is a Mithraic monument, depicting with the usual symbols, the sacrifice of the bull by the young God, a sacrifice which is renewed to this day in the ritual of the bullfight. L'Angloro had drunk of the waters of this fountain and repeats a prophecy she had heard from the old witch who lived there. She interpreted the carvings on the monument to mean that a young man would bring disaster to the river and cause the sailors to be drowned, while the Dra will be driven from the river for ever. This alarms the boatmen for they have heard rumours of fireboats and steamships that can sail up-stream without horses. Thus does the legendary symbolism take on a deeper meaning in this poem which is a hymn to the great river that dominates the poet's country.

The next canto is however still idyllic, as the lovers indulge their dreams, until the calm is shattered by a whistle, and they see pass by a vessel carrying convicts to Toulon: an evil omen. They pass Orange, and arrive at Avignon where there is a diversion in the form of a treasure-hunt, organised by the Venetians. The last part of the eighth and the first part of the ninth canto consist in snatches of conversation, descriptions, and technical matters, until at last the convoy arrives at Beaucaire.

Here the great fair is in full swing, and through its intricacies the lovers wander, in a protracted intermezzo slightly reminiscent of the fair-scene in Gottfried Keller's *Romeo und Julia auf dem Dorfe*, where the lovers, Sali and Vrenchen, are likewise depicted before they are touched by the shadow of tragedy: for romantic love can only be fulfilled by death, by the *Liebestod*.

Meanwhile, the fair and its wares are described in homely detail, until, their business complete, the Condrillots harness the horses to the *Caburle* for the return journey to Lyons. There is a last meal, at which the Prince eulogises the great traditions of the waterway, now threatened, as he instinctively feels; but his words are brave; there is no use lamenting a lost cause, let us rather drink to the Rhône and the harvest sun, let us drink the wine of Genestet despite the vanquishers,

And let the Bull-Rhône bellow in Rouanesso!

Evening is falling as he finishes speaking:

And over Nîmes the sun was going down
And spreading out along the splendid river
The folds of its soft mantle drenched with blood,
And letting fall the last gleam of its rays
Over the Castle of Tarascon whence
King René, at his window, seemed to bless
The Rhône in its supreme and last upheaval.

As the eleventh canto opens, it is dawn, and the ascent begins.
The method of moving upstream is described in detail, and over
all the great figure of Apian presides. He invokes the blessing
of God and the Holy Virgin,

> And under the branches of the white poplars,
> In the silence of the valley of the Rhône,
> And in the splendour of the rising sun,
> Behind the beautiful straining horses
> Who were pouring out vapour from their nostrils,
> The first carter took up the prayer . . .

but although, in this canto, there seems to be a calm, it is only
the calm before the storm, and their prayers are in vain. The
mistral is blowing hard as the last canto opens.

But L'Angloro and Guihèn, oblivious, are talking of the marriage they will celebrate at the foot of the Mithraic monument
at the *font de Tourno;* for they cannot be married as others are:

> Sun of Provence
> O god who brings to birth the grey lizards,
> And calls forth the cicadas from the earth,
> Who in my pallid, melancholy veins
> Brings to life the red blood of my forebears,
> Rhône-god that the Dra in his convolutions
> Entwines at Bourg, at Lyons and at Arles[1]
> And to whom to-day, in the arenas,
> Unconscious sacrifice of the black bull
> Is offered, God who gaily scatters the shadows,
> God whose altar by an unknown shore
> To-day beholds deserted, with its rite
> Abandoned and forgotten—I, a savage,
> I, perhaps the last of your believers,
> Wish to offer on your altar the first-fruits
> Of my happiness, my nuptial night!

The mystic dialogue continues, while, as the climax draws
nearer, the weather calms, the sun appears, and the heat becomes oppressive. The motion of the poem has now become as
sluggish as that of the mighty river, somnolent and menacing.
They have just passed the arches of the Pont St-Esprit when the
first steamboat to be seen upon the Rhône appears suddenly
round a bend, and tears into the line of barges, upsetting them
and their crews, and dragging the horses into the water by which
the whole convoy is swept against the arches of the bridge. When
the Condrillots assemble upon the bank, they have lost their

---

[1] Mithraic shrines.

whole fleet and the Prince and L'Angloro are missing. 'Saint Nicholas has saved our lives', exclaims Apian, 'we will say a mass to him at Condrieu': but *Lou Dra* has carried off L'Angloro to his depths.

The poem ends briefly, on a note of humble resignation, as the survivors, with what they have been able to salvage about them, turn their steps homewards, *senso mai dire*.

On the whole the mixture of elements in this poem is extraordinarily successful. Despite the weight of symbolism which they have to bear, the characters are very real and hold our interest. Some have drawn attention to the 'northern' quality of this work; but, in truth, this quality is not so much northern as gnostic. The love of the principals, and the mithraic symbolism in which the development of the drama is clothed, have a strong gnostic colouring. This flavour, indeed, is strong in Provence, where despite every vicissitude, racial memory is comparatively pure. This flavour is well caught in the lyrical epilogue to Henry de Montherlant's fine novel, *Les Bestiaires*, which is built round a mithraic poem by the Marquis of Baroncelli-Javon. No part of Europe has such a strong association with gnosticism as Languedoc, whither it was brought, in its mithraic form at least, by the Roman soldier, whose works still play a part in the public life of the people. Nowhere has Catholicism been more powerfully touched by local tradition; and Mistral's own faith is inseparable from his patriotism, as can be seen from his attitude to the Albigensians—a gnostic sect—and the Avignonese papacy.

At the same time, as in *Mirèio* the poet restores and rejuvenates the old machinery of the primitive epic by the use of Christian powers, so here, in this poem, he uses to the same end this religious tradition, often associated with the Troubadours, which is still part of the racial consciousness of his people. For this reason alone the fantasy, however irrational, never seems wholly fantastic and, far from being isolated, is merely enhanced by the realistic treatment of the details: the poem is therefore a reading of life, of a true epic breadth, and never a literary exercise, or a poetic *tour de force*.

But, when all is said, the final greatness of this last epic lies in its superb embodiment of a great river, with its life, its moods, its traditions and its inmost character which has influenced for centuries those who live by it: and, if we miss the symmetry and sculpture of *Mirèio*, or the fervent invocations of *Calendau*, we have instead something softer, more mysterious, more melodious; something as reflective as the deep and ever-moving water; something, perhaps, more profound.

For, in *Lou Pouèmo dóu Rose*, the Rhône speaks; and in its pages a mighty river sings forever.

XI

The poet's work was nearly over, but he was to publish one more book of lyrics, *Lis Oulivado* (*The Olive-Gathering*), and a translation of the book of Genesis; and match *Lou Tresor dóu Felibrige* with its physical counterpart, the *Museon Arlaten*, a museum of things Provençal, a 'dictionary of things' as it has been happily called, with the organising and arranging of which he occupied his last years. It was to be the precursor of many regional museums, when other provinces followed his example; and contained furniture, model rooms, clothes, utensils, insects, animals (the Marquis of Baroncelli-Javon gave one of his famous white *Camarguais* horses), paintings and costumes, and was, truly, a 'synthesis of local forces'.

Lis Oulivado appeared in 1912, when Mistral was eighty-two years of age, and as its name implies—for the olive-gathering is the last harvest of the Provençal year—was to be his final word. As he says at the beginning: 'As the weather grows cold and the sea rough, I feel that winter has come for me and that I must without delay gather my olives and offer my virgin oil on God's altar.'

On the whole less impressive than *Lis Isclo d'Or*, it nonetheless contains some great poems, including the sonnet for his own tomb: 'That is the tomb of a poet who fashioned songs for a beautiful Provençale called Mirèio'; and *Evo* (*Eve*) which is a delightful hymn to physical beauty:

> What is the pearl
> That is born of the swirl
> In the kingdom of Amphitrite,
> If it do not shine
> On the ear divine
> Of the pearl-born Aphrodite!

> What are the grains
> The gold-washer gains
> Where the pregnant water swirls,
> If in pretty tresses
> The ore never graces
> Your nape with golden curls!

> What is the rose
> Whose buds unclose
> In the dews of a morning in May,
> If it wake not from sleep,
> If it wake not to weep
> On thy breast that is still more lovely!

What is the cape
That can undrape
Its rainbow's hues in the sky,
If on your whiteness
Its falling brightness
In long folds does not lie!

What is the bait
That makes us elate
With longing to feel thy fire,
If the King of the sky
In his majesty
Has not made thee for desire!

All homage be
To your royalty,
And may all that brings delight,
Smile upon thee
And be offered thee . . .
But never art thou so bright

As in glory's hour
When you burst into flower,
Without dress or finery,
As fateful and bare
As once you were
When God's hand fashioned thee!

In this poem all Mistral's joy and delight in, and his thoroughly Latin love for, the human face and form, the body radiant with the soul that inhabits it, shine forth in all their sweetness.

But perhaps the greatest poem in this collection—and one of the poet's greatest lyrics—is *Lou Parangoun* (*The Archetype*). The Archetype is Provence, which is seen now, through the haze of time, as a great ideal but, like all great ideals, a dream:

My faith is but a dream: that much I know,
But still a dream that seems enveiled in gold,
A honey that can never cease to flow,
A gulf whence I, myself in love, would go
Bearing this Beauty that my arms enfold.

He reviews the forces that play upon this dream which he has raised up to protect his faith against the ambitions, negations and illusions that threaten to devour it.

But in the azure, my pellucid pall,
In the sky's depth and blazing in my eyes,

55

The type of my Provence, the beautiful,
With her breast trembling where the sun's rays fall
And Gyptis' cup in hand, I see arise.

The history of Provence then passes before his eyes:

And now the fair Phoceans she distills,
Crowned with wild olive and with myrtle dark:
Under the cliffs, beneath the wooded hills,
While her sweet song my spellbound hearing fills
As it accompanies the pilot's barque.

Her fortunes rise with Rome, with the Troubadours and the
Courts of Love: at last the Papacy comes to Avignon. And then
begins the sad decline, and all seems lost and buried in dust:

But Santo Estello in the empyrean height
Performed a miracle one fair May morning:
The endless Crau saw bloom in new delight
Mireille—Provence, with Paradise alight,
You've flowered again, fresh fragrance your adorning!

Though all be vanity, and Time pass onward, relentlessly wield-
ing his scythe, faith, at last, is not illusion, but shall have its
reward.

XII

In 1876, Mistral had built a house in Maillane, where he now
lived, an uncrowned king, receiving the homage of visitors from
all over the world. He had become one of the patriarchs he had
so often described in his poems.

In March, 1914, he visited the church to examine a new bell,
and, while there, caught cold. He took to his bed and seemed to
be recovering when, about midday on Lady Day, he became
suddenly worse. His wife sent for the priest. Perhaps he saw the
boat that crossed the sea without a sail, as did his Mirèio, come
to fetch him away, for he spoke the words: 'Li Santo! Li Santo!'
and then he died. He had had a good life. It had passed as
splendidly as the seasons and had been as full and rounded as
the year.

Like that which Mirèio saw break over the Rhône, it had had
its rosy dawn, which had lightened to a blue morning of spring,
such a spring as many a time he had known, when the pastoral
figures of his father and mother moved about among the mul-
berry-trees: for this is the time of the *descoucounavon*. He had had
a perfect childhood and a fortunate youth: his character had
been formed in the classic mould so that, when summer came,

with its *Mirèio* and its *Calendau,* its struggles and its hopes, its gallery of created beings as real as historical figures, its labours in the cause of a region, a language, and a better world, he was able to immortalise it, to pass it on in permanent form, until we who have been less fortunate can dip into those pages as into a clear stream and come forth refreshed by contact with this revelation of the springs of our civilization.

Then came the autumn to this harmonious life. It turned to the river, that flows into the sea as time into eternity, for it was time to reflect: is there not a time for everything under the sun, a time to keep, and a time to cast away? Like those southern evenings he had so often described, when the sun sinks down, folded in its crimson mantle, when the harvesters turn homewards, their purple shadows straying like low-flying birds among the yellow waves of the cornfields; when, like a great wheel, the world turns, drawing up stars out of the sea; when the swans descend, and, red as autumn leaves, the flamingoes dip in salute over the silent meres; as the shadows gathered about him, he poured out the rich reflections of a life-time and then with loving care set his house in order against the coming of winter and darkness.

And at last, as with his own *Meissounié,* the harvest was ripe, and the Harvester came to gather it in.

Frédéric Mistral's life and works form a perfect whole. Mistral is the name, not merely of a noble nature, but of a way of life, a literature, an ideal: through the study of his example and the reading of his work we can return to the sources of that Mediterranean and Latin civilization of which we are such unworthy heirs.

Au noum dóu Felibrige tout entié, Mestre, veici nosti lagremo e tambèn nostis espèr: In the name of the whole Felibrige, Master, behold our tears, and also our hopes.

APPENDIX

p. 11. Cante uno chato de Prouvènço.
   Dins lis amour de sa jouvènço,
A travès de la Crau, vers la mar, dins li bla,
   Umble escoulan dóu grand Oumèro,
   Iéu la vole segui. Coume èro
   Rèn qu'uno chato de la terro,
En foro de la Crau se n'es gaire parla.

p. 12. Dins si quinge an èro Mirèio . . .
   Coustiero bluio de Font-Vièio,
E vous, colo Baussenco, e vous plano de Crau,
   N'avès plus vist de tant poulido!
   Lou gai soulèu l'avié 'spelido;
   E nouveleto, afrescoulido,
Sa caro, à flour de gauto, avié dous pichot trau.

   E soun regard èro uno eigagno
   Qu'esvalissié touto magagno . . .
Dis estello mens dous es lou rai, e mens pur;
   Ié negrejavo de trenello
   Que tout-de-long fasien d'anello;
   E sa peitrino redounello
Èro un pessègue double e panca bèn madur.

p. 12. Vincèn avié sege an pancaro;
   Mai tant dóu cors que de la caro,
Certo, acò' 'ro un bèu drole, e di miéus estampa;
   Emé li gauto proun moureto,
   Se voulès . . . Mai terro negreto
   Adus toujour bono seisseto,
E sort di rasin negre un vin que fai trepa.

p. 13. Cantas, cantas, magnanarello,
   Que la culido es cantarello!
Galant soun li magnan e s'endormon di tres:
   Lis amourié soun plen de fiho
   Que lou bèu tèms escarrabiho,
   Coume un vòu de blóundis abiho
Que raubon sa melico i roumanin dóu gres.

p. 15. Emé si tèsto fièro e libro
   Se revessant dins l'èr que vibro,
Tóuti, d'un meme saut picant la terro ensèn,
   Fasien deja la farandoulo.
   La grand flamado, que gingoulo
   Au revoulun que la ventoulo,
Empuravo à si front de rebat trelusènt.

   Li belugo, à remoulinado,
   Mounton i nivo, aferounado.
Au crussimen di trounc toumbant dins lou brasas

58

Se mesclo e ris la mousiquetto
Dóu flahutet, revertigueto
Coume un sausin dins li branqueto . . .
Sant Jan, la terro aprens trefoulis, quand passas!

La regalido petejavo;
Lou tambourin vounvounejavo,
Grèu e countinuos, coume lou chafaret
De la mar founso, quand afloco
Pasiblamen contro li roco.
Li lamo foro di badoco
E brandussado en l'èr, li dansaire mouret,

Tres fes, à gràndis abrivado,
Fan dins li flamo la Bravado,
E tout en trepassant lou rouge cremadou,
D'un rèst d'aiet trasien li veno
Au recaliéu; e, li man pleno
De trescalan e de verbeno,
Que fasien benesi dins lou fiò purgadou;

Sant Jan! Sant Jan! Sant Jan! cridavon.
Tóuti li colo esbrihaudavon,
Coume s'avié plóugu d'estello dins l'oumbrun.
Enterin la rounflado folo
Empourtavo l'encèns di colo
Emé di fiò la rougeirolo
Vers lou sant, emplana dins lou blu calabrun.

p. 17.   Coume parlavo, dins lou Rose
Tout resplendènt di trelus rose
Que deja lou matin i'espandissié, plan-plan
Mountavo de lahut: di velo
L'auro de mar gounflant la telo,
Li campejavo davans elo
Coume uno pastourello un troupèu d'agnèu blanc.

p. 17. O Sànti Marìo,
Que poudès en flour
Chanja nòsti plour,
Clinas lèu l'auriho
De-vers ma doulour!

Quand veirés, pecaire!
Moun reboulimen
E moun pensamen,
Vendrés de moun caire
Pietadousamen.

Siéu uno chatouno
Qu'ame un jouveinet,
Lou bèn Vincenet!
Iéu l'ame, Santouno,
De tout moun senet!

59

Iéu l'ame! iéu l'ame,
Coume lou valat
Amo de coula,
Coume l'aucèu flame
Amo de voula.

E volon qu'amosse
Aquéu fiò nourri
Que vòu pas mouri!
E volon que trosse
L'amelié flouri!

O Sànti Marìo,
Que poudès en flour
Chanja nòsti plour,
Clinas lèu l'auriho
De-vers ma doulour!

D'alin siéu vengudo
Querre cici la pas.
Ni Crau, ni campas,
Ni maire esmougudo
Qu'arrèste mi pas!

E la souleiado,
Emé si clavèu
E sis arnavèu,
La sènte, à raiado,
Que poun moun cervèu.

Mai, poudès me crèire!
Dounas-me Vincèn;
E gai e risènt,
Vendren vous revèire
Tóuti dous ensèn.

L'estras de mi tempe
Alor calara;
E dóu grand ploura
Moun regard qu'èi trempe,
De gau lusira.

Moun paire s'oupauso
A-n-aquel acord:
De touca soun cor,
Vous èi pau di causo,
Bèlli Santo d'or!

Emai fugue duro
L'óulivo, lou vènt
Que boufo is Avènt,
Pamens l'amaduro
Au poun que counvèn.

60

La nèspo, l'esperbo,
Tant aspro au culi
Que fan tressali,
I'a proun d'un pau d'erbo
Pèr li remouli!

O Sànti Marìo,
Que poudès en flour
Chanja nòsti plour,
Clinas lèu l'auriho
De-vers ma doulour!

p. 21.   ... *amo de maun païs,*

Tu que dardaies, manifèsto,
E dins sa lengo e dins sa gèsto;
Quand li baroun picard, alemand, bourguignoun,
Sarravon Toulouso e Bèu-Caire,
Tu qu'empurères de tout caire
Contro li négri cavaucaire
Lis ome de Marsiho e li fiéu d'Avignoun;

Pèr la grandour di remembranço
Tu que nous sauves l'esperanço;
Tu que dins la jouinesso, e plus caud e plus bèu
Mau-grat la mort e l'aclapaire,
Fas regreia lou sang di paire;
Tu qu'ispirant li dous troubaire,
Fas pièi mistraleja la voues de Mirabèu;

Car lis oundado seculàri
E si tempèsto e sis esglàri
An bèu mescla li pople, escafa li counfin,
La terro maire, la Naturo,
Nourris toujour sa pourtaduro
Dóu meme la: sa pousso duro
Toujour à l'oulivié dounara l'òli fin;

Amo de-longo renadivo,
Ano jouiouso e fièro e vivo,
Qu'endihes dins lou brut dóu Rose e dóu Rousau
Amo di séuvo armouniouso
E di calanco souleiouso,
De la patrìo amo piouso,
T'apelle! encarno-te dins mi vers prouvençau!

p. 23.   Oh! se lou tastavias! L'abiho
N'a pas de mèu plus dous, e briho
Coume un linde diamant, e sènt lou roumaniéu
Emai lou brusc, emai la nerto,
Qu'à nòsti colo fan cuberto,
E danso dins lou vèire ... Certo,
N'escoulariéu un flasco, aro, se lou teniéu.

61

p. 23.　　La niuchado es lindo, estivenco:
　　　　　D'astre à mesuro que s'avenco
　　　　Un revoulun, d'estello un revoulun plus bèu
　　　　Mounto au levant; douço à la remo,
　　　　Courouso e bouleguivo e semo,
　　　　Sèmblo eilalin que la mar cremo . . .
　　　Es un chale, e toujour ié sias que mai nouvèu.

p. 26.　　Aubre dóu mount Gibau! Pinedo,
　　　　　Éusiero, nerto e mourvenedo!
　　　　E tu, soulèu tremount! e tu, càmpèstre siau!
　　　　　E tu, mar superbo! à l'angòni,
　　　　　Vous prene, iéu, pèr testimòni
　　　　　De moun eterne matrimòni! . . .
　　　　Aucèu de la fourèst, cantas lou cant nouviau!

p. 29. Prouvençau, veici la coupo
　　　　Que nous vèn di Catalan:
　　　　A-de-rèng beguen en troupo
　　　　Lou vin pur de noste plant!

p. 30. . . . aubourant sa caro estrafaciado,
　　　　Amudi, desdegnous de la blanco esluciado,
　　　　Arregardo lou Cèu coume fan li dana,
　　　　E pièi à soun trebau retourno entahina.

p. 34. Aubouro-te, raço latino,
　　　　Souto la capo dóu soulèu!
　　　　Lou rasin brun boui dins la tino
　　　　Lou vin de Diéu gisclara lèu.

　　　　Emé toun péu que se desnouso
　　　　A l'auro santo dóu Tabor,
　　　　Tu siés la raço lumenouso
　　　　Que viéu de joio e d'estrambord;
　　　　Tu siés la raço apoustoulico
　　　　Que sono li campano à brand:
　　　　Tu siés la troumpo que publico
　　　　E siés la man que trais lou gran.

　　　　Ta lengo maire, aquéu grand flume
　　　　Que pèr sèt branco s'espandis,
　　　　Largant l'amour, largant lou lume
　　　　Coume un resson de Paradis,
　　　　Ta lengo d'or, fiho roumano
　　　　Dóu Pople-Rèi, es la cansoun
　　　　Que rediran li bouco umano,
　　　　Tant que lou Verbe aura resoun.

＊　＊　＊

　　　　Sus ti coustiero soulciouso
　　　　Crèis l'óulivié, l'aubre de pas,
　　　　E de la vigno vertuiouso

62

S'enourgulisson ti campas:
Raço latino, en remembranço
De toun destin sèmpre courous,
Aubouro-te vers l'esperanço,
Afrairo-te souto la Crous!

p. 35. Grand soulèu de la Prouvènço,
Gai coumpaire dóu mistrau,
Tu qu'escoules la Durènço
Coume un flot de vin de Crau,

Fai lusi toun blound calèu!
Coucho l'oumbro emai li flèu!
Lèu! lèu! lèu!
Fai te vèire, bèu soulèu!

p. 35. De nòsti paire canten la glòri
Que dins l'istòri
An fa soun trau,
E que de-longo, nous dien li libre,
Soun resta libre
Coume la mar e lou mistrau.

p. 36. A passa tèms qu'avian dins la Prouvènço
Un rèi nouma Carle Segound lou Goi;

p. 36. Segnour, avèn, leissant à rèire
Ti sacramen
E mandamen,
Avèn, brutau, plus vougu crèire
Qu'à l'interès
E qu'au Prougrès!

p. 36. E lou vièi meissounié sus la rufo gavello
Èro coucha, tout pale e tout ensaunousi,
E levant soun bras nus que la caud a brounzi,
Parlavo ansin i ligarello.

p. 37. . . . au païs ounte sarai tout-aro,
Me vai èstre de-mau, quand lou sero vendra,
De noun plus, coume antan sus la tepo amourra,
Ausi dóu bèu jouvènt la cansoun forto e claro
Entre lis aubre s'enaura.

p. 37. Dins l'aire tout-d'un-cop si dous bras s'aubourèron,
D'un estrange belu sis iue beluguejèron:
— O mounsegne sant Jan, cridè, sant Jan d'estiéu,
Patroun di meissounié, paire de la pauriho,
Dins voste Paradis souvenès-vous de iéu!

p. 37. Lou vièi s'èro teisa: sis iue toujour fissavon,
Mai soun cors coume un mabre èro devengu blanc;
E mut, li meissounié, lou voulame à la man,

A meissouna se despachavon,
Car un mistrau à flamo espóussavo lou gran.

p. 38. De la pensado crearello
        Pèr tu se desfourrello
        La santo escurita:
    E veses la founsour dis àuti meraviho,
    E dins toun raive d'or plus degun te reviho,
    Car tènes plenamen l'eterno verita.

p. 41. Pereilavan tout blanquinejo,
        Pereilamount tout luminejo.
        E de la colo an bèu pounchoun,
        La tèsto dins soun capuchoun,
        Lou sant ermito es en estàsi.
        En éu la vido es morto quàsi
        E l'amo soulo es en esvèi.
        L'Ange ié parlo, e res lou vèi.
        Mai de l'ermito li prunello
        Veson sis alo blanquinello
        Que, dins l'espàci founs e pur,
    .   En se foundènt emé l'azur,
        An trefouli coume dos velo.

p. 44. Voudriéu dins lou clarun me foundre, se poudiéu!
        Un vaigne sentimen de l'infini de Diéu
        Me pivello . . . La mar es bello, es amourouso,
        Es lindo dins sa glòri, es uno rèino urouso!

p. 47. Van parti de Lioun à la primo aubo
        Li veiturin que règnon sus lou Rose.
        Es uno raço d'ome caloussudo,
        Galoio e brave, li Coundriéulen. Sèmpre
        Planta sus li radèu e li sapino,
        L'uscle dóu jour e lou rebat de l'aigo
        Ié dauron lou carage coume un brounze.
        Mai d'aquéu tèms encaro mai, vous dise,
        Ié vesias d'oumenas à barbo espesso,
        Grand, courpourènt, clapu tau que de chaine,
        Boulegant un saumié coume uno bousco,
        De poupo à pro cridant, jurant de-longo
        E largamen, pèr se baia courage,
        Au poutarras pintant la roujo tencho,
        A bèu taioun tirant la car de l'oulo.
        De-long dóu flume èro uno bramadisso
        Que d'auro en auro entendias de-countùni:
        " Pro vers la baisso, hòu! reiaume! empèri!"
        Amount la pro! dau! fa tira la maio!

p. 48. O tèms di viéi, tèms gai, tèms de simplesso,
        Qu'èro lou Rose un revoulun de vido
        Ounte venian, enfant, sus l'aigo longo
        Vèire passa, fièr, li man à l'empento,
        Li Coundriéulen! Lou Rose, gràci à-n-éli,

64

Èro un grand brusc plen de vounvoun e d'obro.
Tout acò vuei es mort e mut e vaste
E, las! d'aquéu varai tout ço que rèsto
Es lou traçan e la rousigaduro
Que la maio a cava contro li pèiro.

p. 48. Patroun Apian éu-meme sus la poupo
Es au gouvèr que douno l'endrechiero.
A de long péu en cadeneto griso
Que sus li tempe entrena ié retoumbon
Emé dous grand tourtis d'or que ié pènjon
A sis auriho. Es aut de fourcaduro
E, de sis iue lusènt sus chasco barco
Dóu tèms que vèi se tout marcho dins l'ordre,
De l'uno a l'autro, estacado a la filo
Pèr la calaumo unenco e loungarudo,
En escatant dins lou gourgoui de l'aigo
Tóuti li barco à-de-rèng s'entrahinon.

p. 49. . . . es la flour de Rose, moun béu prince,
L'esparganèu que souto l'oundo naiso
E qu'amo tant, l'Angloro, d'ana cueie!

p. 50. – Es éu! es éu! – quilè coume uno folo

p. 50.   Te recounèisse,
O flour de Rose espelido sus l'aigo!
Flour de bonur qu'ai entre-visto en sounge . . .

p. 50. – Te recounèisse, o Dra! Souto la lono
T'ai vist en man l'esparganéu que tènes . . .

p. 50.   Car lis amour van vite,
Uno fes dins la nau que lis emporto,
Predestina, sus lou flot.

p. 50.   Lis arcado
Dóu Pont Sant-Esperit, espetaclouso,
Ié passon en triounfle sus la tèsto . . .
. . . La Prouvènço aparèis: es soun intrado,
Lou Pont Sant-Esperit emé si pielo
E si vint arc superbe que se courbon
En guiso de courouno sus lou Rose.
Acò's la porto santo e courounello
De la terro d'amour. L'aubre d'óulivo,
Lou mióugranié tout fièr de si papàrri
E li gràndi mihiero capeludo
Oundron deja li cremen e li costo.
Lou plan se relargis, li bro verdejon,
Dins lou clarun lou cèu s'emparadiso,
Lis Uba dóu Ventour se laisson vèire . . .

p. 51. E brame lou Rouan, en Rouanesso![1]

p. 51. Or lou soulèu sus Nimes trecoulavo,
Espargissènt an long dóu vaste flùvi
Li ple de sa flassado ensaunousido
E de si rai la reflamour darriero
Sus lou castèu de la Tarasco, mounte
Lou rèi Reinié semblavo, à sa fenèstro,
Benesi la suprèmo rouanado.

p. 52. E souto lou brancun di gràndis aubo,
Dins lou silènci de la vau de Rose,
A l'esplendour dóu soulèu que se lèvo,
Au pas di bèu chivau que s'escourpouiron
E de si narro embandisson la tubo,
Lou proumiè carretié dis la preguiero . . .

p. 52.   Soulèu de la Prouvènço
O diéu que ié coungreies lis angloro,
Que fas sourti d'en terro li cigalo,
Que dins mi veno marfo e palinouso
Reviéndes lou sang rouge de mi rèire,
Diéu roudanen que lou Dra dins si vòuto
Agouloupo, à Lioun, au Bourg, en Arle,
E que dóu negre tau dins lis Areno
Encaro vuei t'es fa lou sacrifice
Incounsciènt, diéu qu'escavartes l'oumbro
Galoi, qu'en uno ribo incouneigudo
Vuei es desert toun autar – e toun rite
Abandouna dins l'óublid, iéu barbare,
Iéu lou darrié bessai de ti cresèire,
Vole sus toun autar óufri, premiço
De ma felicita, ma niue de noço! –

p. 54.   Qu'es la perlo
        Qu'en bousserlo
Se coungreio au founs di nàis,
        Se noun briho
        A l'auriho
L'Afroudito que ié nais!

        Qu'es l'or lèime
        Qu'à bèl èime
L'arpaiaire vai culi,
        S'en trenello
        Roussinello
A toun cou noun vèn pali!

        Qu'es la roso
        Que s'arroso
Eme l'eigagnau de Mai,

---

[1] Rouan is the bull, a symbolic name for the Rhône, and *Rouanesse* a part of Beaucaire, from *Rhodanusia*, an old Greek colony.

66

Se noun flouro
E noun plouro
Sus toun sen que flouro mai!

Qu'es la raubo
Que derraubo,
Si coulour a l'arcoulan,
Se noun pènjo
E noun rènjo
Si long ple sus toun cors blanc!

Qu'es la morso
Que nous forço
De bela vers ta cremour,
Se lou mèstre
Dóu celèstre
Noun t'a facho pèr l'amour!

Oumenage
Au reinage,
Tout ço que i'a d'esclatant,
Qu'à tu rigue
E s'óufrigue . . .
Mai siés bello jamai tant

Coume en glòri
Quand fas flòri,
Sènso faudo ni faudiéu,
Lindo! talo
Que, fatalo,
Te pastè la man de Diéu!

p. 55. Ma fe n'es qu'un pantai: acò, lou sabe.
Mai lou pantai me sèmblo embruma d'or,
Me sèmblo un mèu que iéu jamai acabe,
Me sèmblo un gourg d'ounte amourous derrabe
Sus mi dous bras la bello que ié dor.

p. 55. Mai dins l'azur tant clar que m'encapello
Aut que-noun sai, à mis iue resplendis
Lou parangoun de ma Prouvènço bello
Emé soun piés qu'au soulèu reboumbello
E dins sa man la coupo de Giptis.

p. 56. Quouro retrais li dono de Foucido
Se courounant de nerto e d'óulivié:
Au pèd di baus, di colo agarrussido,
Soun dous soulòmi encanto moun ausido,
Acoumpagnant la barco dóu prouvié.

p. 56. Mai santo Estello au soun de l'Empirèio
A fa miracle, un bèu matin de Mai:
La vasto Crau vèi espeli Mirèio
E dins lou cèu, o Prouvènço, en idèio
As reflouri, mai flòri que jamai . . .

CHRONOLOGICAL TABLE

1830. Mistral born at Maillane.
1854. Birth of the Felibrige.
1858. First reading of *Mirèio*.
1859. *Mirèio* published at Avignon.
1866. *Calendau.*
1867. Visit to Paris with Balaguer.
1874. Festival in honour of Petrarch, at Avignon.
1878. The Floral Games, at Montpellier.
1878. *Lis Isclo d'Or*, revised edition.
    Lou Tresor dóu Felibrige.
    Nerto.
1890. *La Rèino Jano.*
1891. Appearance of *L'Aioli.*
1897. *Lou Pouèmo dóu Rose.*
1912. *Lis Oulivado.*
1914. Mistral dies at Maillane.

LIST OF MISTRAL'S WORKS

Mirèio
Calendau
Lis Isclo d'Or
Lou Tresor dóu Felibrige
Nerto
La Rèino Jano
Lou Pouèmo dóu Rose
Moun Espelido, Memòri e Raconte (Memoirs)
Discours e Dicho (Speeches)
La Genèsi (Genesis)
Lis Oulivado
Escourregudo Per l'Itali (Letters from Italy)
Proses d'Almanach (3 volumes)
La Gerbe de Mistral à l'Autel de Marie

ENGLISH TRANSLATIONS

Mireille, H. Crichton, London, 1868 (verse).
Mirèio, H. W. Preston, London, 1890; Boston, 1891 (verse).
    „   C. H. Grant, London, undated (prose).
Memoirs, C. E. Maud, London and New York, 1907.
Anglore (*Lou Pouèmo dóu Rose*), Maro Beath Jones, California, 1937 (verse).